HOW IT ALL BEGAN

Bommi Baumann

WIE ALLES ANFING

Translated by
Helene Ellenbogen & Wayne Parker

HOW IT ALL BEGAN

The Personal Account

of a West German

Urban Guerrilla

ARSENAL PULP PRESS
VANCOUVER

WIE ALLES ANFING
HOW IT ALL BEGAN

Copyright © 1975 Trikont Verlag, Munich
Copyright © 1977 Pulp Press, for the English Translation
Copyright © 1981 Pulp Press, 2nd Edition
Copyright © 2000 Arsenal Pulp Press, Revised 2nd Edition

THIRD PRINTING: 2018

ARSENAL PULP PRESS
#202 – 211 East Georgia St.
Vancouver, BC V6A 1Z6
Canada
arsenalpulp.com

Printed and bound in Canada

ISBN: 978-0-88978-045-3

Contents

PUBLISHER'S NOTE:
Michael Baumann was arrested in London, England, in February, 1981. As this edition goes to press (April '81) we understand that he is being held in a prison in West Berlin. We have been unable to obtain further details.

Foreword to the 2nd Edition

When *Wie Alles Anfing* was released in Munich in September 1975, it caused an almost unprecedented storm of controversy, both among the German authorities who wanted to suppress it and in many left circles, who saw it as sedition against the revolutionary movement.

At that time Germany was reeling from the Lorenz kidnapping, in which Baumann's former comrades quite cleverly traded the freedom of a prominent conservative political figure for the release of five imprisoned urban guerillas. The "second generation" of the Red Army Fraction and the June 2nd Movement was just going into high gear.

In the three years that followed, the West German state and the urban guerilla movement waged a steadily escalating war on each other. The state, with the enthusiastic assistance of the news media, systematically attacked the entire left so viciously and thoroughly that a Bertrand Russell International Tribunal was convened in 1978 to investigate widespread crimes against human rights in the Federal Republic. The guerilla groups, while not without some spectacular successes, were losing a steady war of attrition during this period. While outside support dwindled as a result of fear and legal prosecution, the guerillas were dying in shootouts, being arrested, imprisoned, and not infrequently "suicided" in their isolation cells.

It is this series of developments that forces us to re-examine Baumann's critique. For him, the outcome of the struggle was predetermined by the forms of organization and action which it had adopted. What began with illegality and clandestinity among a group of friends ended in the continual narrowing of the community of comrades and the professionalization of all their activities. What began with the joyful rebellion against oppression ended with isolation from society, internally imposed pressure to produce and achieve, and led inexorably to imprisonment, nervous collapse, betrayals and death. Most significantly, it also led to the destruction of the vision of a new life which had inspired the revolution in the beginning.

After Baumann, others too found the same problems and arrived at the same conclusions. In secret interviews with journalists, Hans Joachim Klein (of OPEC raid fame) described how he suddenly found himself no longer an independent actor in a revolutionary project of his own creation, but merely a pawn, a mercenary in a game of global power struggle. This total loss of control over the role one plays in the revolutionary project is the logical outcome of the institutionalization of armed struggle as the property of vanguard groups vying for power with the state, as both Baumann and Klein eventually realized.

The story of what happened to the larger movement from which the guerilla groups emerged is also worth noting. The trend toward increasingly repressive laws and institutions was already quite noticeable by the beginning of the 1970's. But the "German Autumn" of 1977, during and after the kidnapping of Hans Martin Schleyer, was a nightmare example of systematic state terror in the modern world. It represented a clear breaking point, the end of an era.

There would continue to be sporadic bombings, and fugitive guerillas would still occasionally manage a desperate bank robbery, but it was clear that the organizations were crippled and the remaining members on the run. In the meantime, it was over a year before the terrorized legal segments of the revolutionary movement were able to pull themselves together, to appear again on the streets and in their communities, to publicly pose once again in a militant way the question of the revolutionary alternative to German "progress" and "order".

What happened in Germany was hardly unique. In Italy, just a few months after Schleyer and Mogadischu, the closing act of the revolutionary play of the 60's and 70's was re-enacted almost identically in the Red Brigades' kidnapping of Aldo Moro. There too, the fate of one man's life became an overriding symbol, diminishing any other significance of the action. And there too, the drama became the pretext for an all-out assault on the left.

In the United States, the era went out more with a fizzle than a bang. The Weather Underground quietly turned themselves in during the past two years, after years of inactivity and a concerted move toward the most rigid forms of Leninism. The SLA, after its short months of spectacular news coverage, fell victim to the same forces Baumann described: isolation, loss of contact with reality, and police terror. After the SLA, there were a few imitator groups across the country, but a conspiracy of silence had set in among the news media. So they were denied even their small moments of heroism and acclaim. By the late 1970's, the militant left out of which these groups emerged had itself almost disappeared.

Why, then, this new edition of Baumann's story? When *Wie Alles Anfing* was released in 1975, and indeed when we translated it in 1977, the book was a critique of contemporary events which were still in progress. Clearly that generation, the 60's and their aftermath in the 70's, is now over. What remains is for us to analyze that history and to find in it a means and an understanding to create a future.

The brave new world we have entered over the past decades is a world dominated by the images of death. We have sudden death in the form of impending nuclear warfare; lingering death in the form of environmental degradation; massive death by starvation; self-inflicted death in the cults; deliberate death for the revolution; accidental death on the highways and in the factories; death by boredom and death by loneliness.

Baumann's story is the tale of a survivor. Like many among us, he turned away from the shoddy representation of revolution as another road to death. Like many among us, he began to build a new vision of revolution based on life, on love, on joy and on creativity. There are moments in his book when we can catch glimpses of that kind of life, moments when the activity of the revolution becomes a festival of communal activity, when wit becomes more powerful than the arm of the state, when love and friendship are the adhesive of resistance to the drab blue of the police and the culture of death.

We have no illusions that violence and destruction can be avoided in the years ahead. As Baumann said, "violence is a perfectly adequate means, I never had any hangups about it". But we must learn now to distinguish between an act within the *modus operandi* and the total means, and we must learn to understand that the means is the end and not simply a justification for it. Thus Baumann's exhortation that we commit ourselves to building communities of life to sustain us in the difficult times ahead, that we widen our experiences and collective possibilities and that we live now as closely to that vision of life after the revolution as is possible, is more valid than ever.

We, as well as that younger generation now reaching maturity with the history of the 60's and 70's as their immediate reference, would do well to learn from that history. We need to escape the fate which has plagued so many generations of our predecessors, the doom of repeating the same mistakes, of buying the same thinly-veiled illusions. We need to invent a new vocabulary of struggle, one without coercion and without hierarchy. We need to discover new forms of organization, new architectures for our cities and new environments for our lives. We need to experiment with lives based on joy and not on technology, and we need to taste, even if only for a moment, the spices and ambrosia of a new freedom free of compulsion and restraints from within ourselves.

So for us, Baumann's book is a link between our history and our future. And we reprint it, in that spirit, with the hope that wherever he is and wherever we are, the sun and the sea will cleanse us of the past and strengthen us for the future.

Helene Ellenbogen
Wayne Parker

Introduction

On November 24th, 1975, thirty policemen armed with sub-machine guns burst into the offices of *Trikont Verlag*, a Munich publishing house and, holding the six staff members present at gunpoint, proceeded to search and ransack the place. They took photographs, broke open doors and cabinets, entered adjoining private rooms, body-searched all present and confiscated personal letters and address books. In addition to the Trikont offices they searched (without warrant) the upstairs premises of a women's publishing collective and also the home of an immigrant worker and his family who were living in a back wing of the building and who were completely terrified by the experience. During this time the Trikont people were not permitted access to an attorney or to inform their office manager who was absent. When they made coffee or went to the bathroom they were escorted at gunpoint. The search lasted five hours. When the police left they took with them 1600 books, all the office typewriters, typesetting equipment, files, subscription lists, publicity material, tapes, mailing lists, bank statements and sales receipts. The office was bare and *Trikont* was effectively put out of operation at the height of the pre-Christmas book season.

Trikont Verlag is a small publisher of a fairly broad spectrum of left-oriented books and materials. The object of this massive police operation against it was a book it had published some months earlier: *Wie Alles Anfing* (How it all Began), a personal memoire by Michael "Bommi" Baumann who, at the time, was one of the 14 most wanted terrorists in West Germany. The raid secured only 300 copies of the desired text (the rest of the 1600 books taken consisting of other, non-related *Trikont* titles). Subsequent raids, on two book distributors in West Berlin, on one in Frankfurt and on two bookstores in Hanover, netted another 200 copies—hardly enough to stop circulation and keep the books from being read but enough to throw a scare into anyone involved in the writing or publication of texts to do with violence or terrorism or further means of direct action against the state. The raid on *Trikont* and the ensuing court action around *Wie Alles Anfing* became, on the one hand, a cause for outrage and public debate over questions of freedom of expression and state repression of ideas and, on the other, a test case for the new book censorship laws which were, at the time, being discussed in the West German Parliament. It also pushed a book which might otherwise have had a fairly restricted readership— the initial press run was 3000 copies—into the international limelight.

Wie Alles Anfing is the straightforward and quite personal story of Michael Baumann's development from a working class building apprentice into an urban guerrilla. For those of us in North America to whom the "phenomenon" of European terrorism is at first sight somewhat perplexing and not entirely consistent with our own understanding of the evolutionary processes which radical movements from the sixties have, or should have, undergone, it is a revealing document. It is one thing to note that the radical *forms* and *gestures* which America exported to Europe during these tumultuous years were eagerly taken up and utilized by the European revolutionaries; it is another to realize that these forms and gestures acquired, gradually, a new *content* in the concrete circumstances of the European situation and eventually spawned a mode of revolutionary expression which remained at a fairly rudimentary stage in the North American context.

From 1969 (approximately) until 1972 Michael Baumann was a leading member of the June 2nd Movement, one of the most active urban guerrilla groups in West Berlin (please see chronology) and one which is still active today—albeit without Baumann. In this book he explains how he got there, names the forces that drove him, fairly systematically and logically, into an extreme radicalism and into violence. Although it is not necessarily typical (and Baumann makes no claim that it is) his story nevertheless goes a long way in explaining for us some of the personal truths and pressures which have spawned the current proliferation of terrorist organizations in Europe.

It begins with him as the young apprentice—a "perfectly normal person," as he describes himself—from a broken home in one of the ugly low-cost housing developments on the outskirts of Berlin. Because he likes long hair he is harrassed at home, in the streets and on the job-site. To console himself he listens to rock'n'roll and reads books, goes to the bar and gets into fights. One day, on the way to work, seeing the daily treadmill stretching out endlessly before him, his mind snaps and he flees into the city. There he becomes involved in the street scene, the dope scene and eventually the student scene and movement which is erupting out into the West Berlin streets. The police shooting of Benno Ohnesorg (a Berlin student) during a demonstration (on June 2nd, 1967) and especially the right-wing assassination attempt on student leader Rudi Dutschke during Easter 1968 are the events which consolidate Baumann's *political* radicalization.

For North Americans it is often difficult to fathom the close connection that existed in Germany—and especially in the island of West Berlin—between the "political" scene and the "counter-culture" scene. American pop radicalism took on a somewhat more sombre face when it arrived in this besieged city and it was only natural that, on moving into one of the first "communes" in West Berlin (the K.I.) Baumann should begin mixing politics and dope, "trips" and police beatings, "highs" and violence in a manner not generally conceived of by the broadstream, white American student Left. Add to this the fact that Baumann came from a working class background where violence was an almost daily presence—fights in the bar; street beatings; watching his father come home drunk on payday and beat up his mother—and we begin to see the roots of his radicalism and to understand his subsequent actions. For Baumann and his comrades the model for action became the American Black Panther Movement and it was in the K.1 that they began constructing their first bombs and planning their first bank robberies.

The rest of the book describes the various actions, the resulting analysis, the criticisms and eventual development of the June 2nd Movement with its call to pick up the gun. Baumann is always clear, he is always critical and he is always honest. The latter chapters where he describes the harsh realities of living outside the law—where every "illegal" person needs a "legal" one to take care of him; where the vicious circle of violence freezes all personal relationships; where ones' lovers are ruthlessly interrogated and made to inform—are recommended reading for those to whom the image of the urban terrorist is still a somewhat romantic and vaguely desirable one. Here lies the strength of this book, and its importance for us here in North America — where the romantic image of the terrorist as desperado, criminal or outlaw is daily sold across the counter: Baumann gives the "phenomenon" a human face, places it in the context of real events and historical forces and thus helps us to understand why terrorism — be it the R.A.F., be it the Red Brigades, or the June 2nd Movement — is being practiced by certain people. And in so doing he does much to undercut those current headlines which serve, so often, to further mystify terrorism and its presence among us, and to eventually mystify violence itself.

In this book Michael Baumann is being allowed to talk, to talk openly and freely about his own experiences and from his own unique position. That, in many ways, is a victory. The issue here is definitely violence: who uses it, who should be allowed to use it and should the state have a monopoly on its use. These are legal and also political questions. There is the further question, however, of whether or not a person who has admitted to terrorist acts should be allowed free expression. This is a question for every reader of this current volume.

The legal grounds for the police raid on *Trikont Verlag* were two clauses in the West German criminal code which define the "support of punishable acts" and the "presentation of materials glorifying violent acts or rendering them insignificant" as criminal activities. The charges against *Trikont* were initially dismissed but the decision was later overturned in appeal court proceedings. The on-going case against *Trikont* and against this book must, however, be seen in relation to concurrent parliamentary debates around them and the passing, in January 1976, of the "Law for the Protection of Communal Peace." This law (popularly termed the "muzzle law") makes it a crime, punishable by imprisonment up to a year "to distribute, openly exhibit, post, introduce, otherwise make accessible, or produce, supply, keep in storage, offer or advertise, writing depicting violence to humans of a gruesome or otherwise inhuman sort, thereby glorifying such acts or rendering them insignificant." As a piece of censorship legislation this is the tightest in Germany since the Nazi book-burning days. It has given police and the courts wide-ranging powers of discretion and led to numerous clamp-downs on predominantly left-wing publishers and publications. It is also the law under which, in the spring of 1978, the *Trikont* editors were convicted for the publication of the Baumann book.

The muzzle law works in concert with other recent legislation. Germany is currently experiencing a wave of reaction against terrorism and the resulting restrictions of civil liberties and freedom of speech are the most severe of any western democracies. The "support of anti-constitutional behavior" or the "encouragement of anti-constitutional behavior" are now crimes in West Germany. Terms such as "enemy of the Constitution" and "contravening the spirit of the Constitution" have crept into the legal vocabulary. The job-ban decrees have led to wide-spread blacklisting of persons "suspected" of having engaged in left-wing activities. A climate of fear and reprisal— heated up tremendously by such events as the Schleyer kidnapping and death, the Mogadischu raid and the prison deaths of Andreas Baader, Gudrun Ensslin and Jan-Carl Raspe—is now the order of the day in West Germany and it is this climate in to which the on-going debate around this book falls.

In the spring of 1976 *Trikont* responded to police efforts to suppress the Baumann text by coming out with a second edition of 10,000 copies. Three hundred sixty people and groups— including such notables as Sartre and Heinrich Böll—signed it as co-publishers. This effectively halted further action against the book and, although the case against *Trikont* continued, Baumann was freely available in bookstores all over Europe. Translations into Dutch, Swedish, Italian and three further languages soon followed. The first English language edition appeared in Vancouver, Canada, in the fall of 1977.

It is clear that what Baumann has to say is important and sought-after by many people who wish to look behind the headlines on terrorism which are taking up more and more space in our newspapers and newscasts. And—quite apart from the question of the legality or illegality of Baumann's violent acts— the effort to suppress and make *the saying of it* illegal may turn out, in the long run, to be itself an act of violence.

Finally, a word on the translation: Baumann's German is a unique mixture of Berlin dialect, American slang, and social science jargon. It is the street language which the post-war generation of young Germans inherited from their parents, from the American occupation and from the student movement. It is, quite deliberately, a language which cannot be easily understood by an older generation of Germans. It incorporates a host of American expressions directly and the effect of this is of course lost on translating these "back" into English. The translators have striven for clarity of content while trying to maintain the informality and free-flow, the run-on sentence structure and rapid shift of tenses which characterize Baumann's speech. The effect, hopefully, is an authentic, human, spoken tone which will give back some of the flavour, if not all the subtleties, of the original.

Pulp Press
Vancouver, July 1978

Note: The German publishers were unable to provide source information for the newspaper and magazine reports, pamphlets and posters presented in facsimile at the end of each chapter. This material was seized in the police raid, and never returned. *(Ed.)*

Chronology

Early 1967   Micahel "Bommi" Baumann joins the German Socialist Student Group (S.D.S.) in Berlin. Soon thereafter, he joins Kommune 1 (K.1), the first publically known German commune.

June 2, 1967   Benno Ohnesorg, a student demonstrating against the Shah of Iran in West Berlin, is fatally wounded by a policeman, Karl Heinz Kurras.

Easter, 1968   Following an attempt by right-wing assassins on the life of Rudi Dutschke, a leading spokesman of the German New Left, demonstrations and rioting accompanied by arson and bombings take place throughout West Germany. Michael Baumann is arrested for slashing automobile tires and sentenced to nine months imprisonment.

April 2, 1968   In Frankfurt, four people set a major department store on fire. The group, which is apprehended, includes Andreas Baader, Gudrun Ensslin, and two others who later form the Red Army Fraction (R.A.F.)

February 27, 1969   Richard Nixon's visit to West Berlin sparks demonstrations, and an unsuccessful bombing attempt on his motorcade. Following the visit, German Security Police raid several Berlin communes, discovering a bomb in one. Dieter Kunel and Rainer Longhans are arrested. The bomb itself had been supplied by the Security Police through an agent provocateur, Peter Urbach.

Summer 1969   The Central Committee of the Roaming Hash Rebels—"militant kernel of Berlin's counter-culture"—is formed. Michael Baumann is one of the group's active members.

July 5, 1969   Berlin's first smoke-in is held, sponsored by the Central Committee of Roaming Hash Rebels.

Fall, 1969   Tupamaros West Berlin (T.W.), West Germany's first urban guerrilla group, is formed. Within a few months a similar group, Tupamaros Munich (T.M.) is also formed.

December 16, 1969   The first political arrest warrants are issued for three suspects in recent political bombings. All three suspects, who are Bernard Braun, Michael Baumann, and an unidentified Dutchman, go underground.

February, 1970   Several anarchists, including Michael Baumann, Thomas Weisbecker, Georg von Rauch, and others, are arrested while beating up Horst Rieck in his Berlin apartment. Rieck, the Berlin correspondent for the illustrated *Quick,* had recently published a scandalous story about political bombings and the New Left in Berlin. Baumann is held for a year and a half; the others are released shortly after the arrest.

May 14, 1970 Andreas Baader is broken out of the Tegel Prison by several armed comrades, including Ulrike Meinhof. An elderly guard is badly wounded in the escape. The escape marks the beginning of the Red Army Fraction.

July 8, 1971 During the trial of Thomas Weisbecker, Michael Baumann, and Georg von Rauch for the assault on Horst Rieck, Baumann and Weisbecker are released on bail. When the release is announced, von Rauch, who is facing a probable ten year sentence on other charges, pretends to be Weisbecker, leaves the courtroom with Baumann, and immediately goes underground. Weisbecker then reveals his identity and is also released. Following the escape, the June 2nd Movement is formed.

December 4, 1971 During a massive search throughout the city of West Berlin following the discovery of a R.A.F. safehouse, three members of the June 2nd Movement get into a shootout with a plainclothes policeman. Georg von Rauch is killed; Michael Baumann and another guerrilla manage to escape, after several hours of pursuit through the city.

January, 1972 The so-called "anti-radical measures" precipitate orders-in-council requiring all persons working on public payroll in West Germany to "actively uphold and maintain, both on and off duty, the basic principles of the B.D.R. Constitution." Nation-wide witch hunts ensue and blacklists begin actively circulating.

February 2, 1972 The June 2nd Movement bombs the British Yacht Club in Kladow. Irwin Beelitz, a 66-year-old German Boatbuilder, is accidentally killed in the blast.

March 2, 1972 Thomas Weisbecker killed in Augsberg in a shootout with two Munich policemen who have just received special training in combat shooting. Carmen Roll is arrested while trying to flee.

April 19, 1972 Four hundred police raid the "Georg von Rauch House", a commune in the Kreuzberg occupied since December, 1971, by working-class youths. Evidence related to recent bombings is discovered, but members of the June 2nd Movement who had been living there under false identities are elsewhere at the time of the raid. Twenty-seven people are taken in for questioning.

June 1, 1972 Andreas Baader, Holger Meins, and Jan-Carl Raspe are wounded and arrested after a shootout in Frankfurt. Gudrun Ensslin and Ulrike Meinhof are arrested shortly thereafter.

Late 1972 Michael Baumann drops out of the June 2nd Movement, but remains underground.

June 4, 1974 Ulrich Schmuecker, a former member of the June 2nd Movement, is assassinated. The assassination is alleged to have been carried out by the June 2nd Movement after Schmuecker informed on the group.

November 9, 1974   Holger Meins, a R.A.F. prisoner since 1972, dies after a two-month hunger strike undertaken to demonstrate prison conditions faced by R.A.F. political prisoners. Demonstrations break out throughout West Germany following the death.

November 10, 1974   Guenter von Drenkman, president of West Berlin's highest court, is assassinated by several members of the June 2nd Movement. In the wake of this action and the demonstrations following the death of Holger Meins, a nationwide sweep is carried out by the Security Police. An R.A.F. safehouse containing explosives, submachine guns, and floor plans of U.S. military installations is found, and at least 20 people are arrested.

November 29, 1974   Ulrike Meinhof is sentenced to 8 years in prison.

February 27, 1975   Peter Lorenz, C.D.U. candidate for Mayor of West Berlin, is kidnapped by the June 2nd Movement three days before the elections. The June 2nd Movement demands the release of 6 imprisoned guerrillas in exchange for Lorenz: Rolf Pohl, Rolf Heissler, Gabriel Kroecher-Tiedman, Horst Mahler, Ina Siepman, and Verena Becher.

March 3, 1975   Four of the imprisoned guerrillas are flown to Frankfurt with Heinrich Albertz, former Mayor of West Berlin, as hostage. The fifth, Gabriel Kroecher-Tiedman, joins them after deciding to accept the release. Horst Mahler refuses to be exchanged.

March 4, 1975   Lorenz released unharmed by the June 2nd Movement. He received 43% of the vote in the mayoral election, but lost the election, which was held while he was captive.

April 25, 1975   Six heavily armed members of the Holger Meins Commandos invade the West German embassy in Stockholm, Sweden. They demand the release of 26 political prisoners, including R.A.F. members imprisoned at Stammheim. Following the German government's refusal to negotiate, and the retaliatory executions of the German military and economic attaches, an accidental explosion of the guerrillas' arsenal ends the episode. One guerrilla and one hostage die in the explosion; the other guerrillas, former members of the Socialist Patients' Collective (S.P.K.), are captured.

April 30, 1975   Four suspects in the Lorenz kidnapping are arrested, including Ronald Fritzsch, Gerald Kloepper, Hendrik Reinders, and Paul Reverman.

June 6, 1975   Till Meyer is wounded and arrested in a shootout with police in West Berlin.

September 9, 1975   Ralf Reinders, Inge Viett, and Julianne Plambeck are arrested. All three are suspects in the Lorenz kidnapping, and Reinders is also wanted in connection with the assassination of von Drenkman.

Autumn, 1975   Trikont Verlag in Munich publishes Michael Baumann's autobiography *Wie Alles Anfing*.

November 24, 1975   Trikont is raided by a task force of some 40 police and political prosecutors armed with submachine guns and search warrants. All available copies of the book are seized, as well as practically everything else in the publishing house. Following this raid, similar confiscations occur in left bookstores throughout West Germany.

January, 1976   West German Parliament passes censorship law under which the writing, production, publication, distribution, advertising, sale, or display of materials "glorifying or encouraging violent acts" is a criminal offence and subject to jail terms of up to three years.

Spring, 1976   *Wie Alles Anfing* is reprinted, following an international campaign against the confiscation of the first printing. A list of 380 co-publishers, including well-known left intellectuals, groups, bookstores, and individuals, appears on the covers.

May 9, 1976   Ulrike Meinhof is found hanged in her prison cell. The West German government and the press immmediately label it as a "Suicide"; subsequent coroner's testimony, however, indicates a possibility that she had been raped and then murdered by strangulation.

May 10, 1976   In Paris, two West German firms, Kloeckner Ina-France and Thyssen-France are bombed in response to Meinhof's death. Major demonstrations take place throughout West Germany, notably in Frankfurt and West Berlin. The following day, the U.S. Armed Forces radio station in West Germany is bombed.

July 7, 1976   Four women convicted or accused of terrorism escape from their maximum security prison by overpowering a guard with a lead pipe, then going over the prison wall. The women are Inge Viett, Gabriele Rollnik, Julianne Plambeck, and Monika Berberich. All except Berberich are under suspicion of having carried out the kidnapping of Lorenz. Several days later, West Berlin Justice Minister Hermann Oxfort resigns in the face of a governmental uproar over the escape.

September 28, 1976   Seven members of Red Army Fraction sentenced to prison terms of 2 to 7 years for fire-bombing deaths in 1970-72.

October 7, 1976   The West German government prosecutor asks for life sentences for R.A.F. members Andreas Baader, Gudrun Ensslin, and Jan-Carl Raspe.

October 27, 1976   Trikont editors are acquitted of charges relating to the first publication of *Wie Alles Anfing*. The prosecution immediately appeals the case.

January 21, 1977   Court orders return of confiscated copies of first edition of "Wie Alles Anfing."

April 8, 1977   West German Federal Prosecutor Siegfried Buback assassinated in Karlsruhe on his way to work. Buback, chief political prosecutor in the B.R.D., was responsible for all prosecutions of suspected terrorists, including the R.A.F members still on trial. Buback and the driver of his Mercedes-Benz limousine are killed immediately, and his bodyguard seriously wounded, when the rider on the back seat of a motorcycle opens fire with a submachine gun. The successful assassination is claimed by the Ulrike Meinhof Action Group.

July 30, 1977   Juergen Ponto, president of West Germany's largest bank, is shot and killed in his mansion in suburban Frankfurt during a kidnapping attempt by the R.A.F.. One of the guerrillas, Susanne Albrecht, is identified as the daughter of close friends of the Ponto family.

August 9, 1977   German Federal Court of Appeal overturns lower court decision and reinstitutes charges against Trikont editors for publication of *Wie Alles Anfing*.

September 5, 1977   Hanns-Martin Schleyer, head of the German Industry Association and a board member of Daimler-Benz, is kidnapped from his limousine in Cologne by the R.A.F. During the kidnapping, Schleyer's driver and three bodyguards are killed by machinegun fire from the R.A.F. members. Schleyer, in addition to being Germany's top industrialist, is a former officer in Hitler's S.S.

October 18, 1977   The hijacking of a Lufthansa jet to Mogadishu, Somalia by Palestinian guerrillas, intended to force the West German government to release imprisoned R.A.F. members, is thwarted by a commando assault on the plane by the German Border Protection Group 9, an anti-terrorist team. A few hours later, the government announces the suicides of Andreas Baader, Gudrun Ensslin, and Jan-Carl Raspe, and the "attempted suicide" of Irmgard Moeller, in the Stammheim Prison. In succeeding days, radicals across Europe bomb and burn German businesses in retaliation for the suspected murders of the three R.A.F. members.

Octoberf 20, 1977   The body of Hanns-Martin Schleyer is discovered in a French border town in the trunk of a car. The R.A.F. claims his execution is in retaliation for the three deaths at Stammheim. In the next few days, a massive hunt is launched across Europe for 18 suspected members of the German underground, and many other radicals are interrogated and arrested as terrorist suspects or sympathizers.

November 12, 1977   Ingrid Schubert, an imprisoned guerrilla whose release had also been demanded by the Mogadishu hijackers, is found hanged in her cell in Munich. Her death provokes further demonstrations and guerrilla actions by R.A.F. supporters across Europe.

May 27, 1978   Two women, believed to be members of the June 2nd Movement, enter the Moabit Prison in West Berlin with lawyers' identity cards. Once inside, they draw pistols and demand the release of

Till Meyer and Andreas Vogel, June 2nd members on trial for bank robberies and the von Drenkmann and Lorenz actions. A guard grabs a gun and locks Vogel in a cell, but the two women and Meyer, after shooting one hostage guard in the leg, force the guards to open the gates. The three then walk to freedom under the eyes of several passing police patrols.

CHAPTER ONE

How It All Began

Before the Extraparliamentary Opposition (A.P.O.) or anything else like it existed, I was a perfectly normal person, a completely well-adjusted apprentice. Before that I was a schoolboy.

We came from East Germany when I was about twelve, and here in the West I had to repeat a year of school because we were moving around. Then I took the practical branch—that is, I did grammar school through the eighth grade and then left and took an apprenticeship as a construction worker. Then I quit my apprenticeship, did all sorts of shit jobs until around '65, when my story starts to be not so conformist anymore. Actually, with me it all began with rock music and long hair. There were the Beatles, Stones, Byrds, and so on. The Them too. I didn't just listen to rock, but blues too, like John Lee Hooker, and guys like that.

At that time in Berlin there were only a few places to hang out: so-called hippy joints like Gammlertreffen, Gedächtniskirche, Dicke Wirtin, Seeschlösschen or Top Ten. Straight places like Big Apple or Eden weren't places you went. In '65 there were teenage dances with school-girls in their white knee-highs.

So that's where my story opens. As long as you fit in, you don't get hassled. You have felt this instinctive reaction against stress, against the pressure to achieve. Since you're in the system, you go along with it automatically, because you don't know anything else and don't see anything else, and you don't have any alternatives. You don't really know what you could do differently.

In my case, at the beginning in Berlin, it was like this: if you had long hair, things were suddenly like they are for the Blacks. Do you understand? They threw us out of joints, they cursed at us and ran after us—all you had was trouble*. You got fired

*'Trouble' is a word Bommi uses in English. The use of English words in the original text is striking in its frequency. Many are taken from song lyrics.

from your job, or you couldn't even get one; or you got these really disgusting jobs, or clearly underpaid ones, and constant hassles with complete strangers on the street. But I was a perfectly normal person. With me it was like this: you suddenly see the connection between yourself and blues music and the problems that surface there, like the situation with the Blacks. And suddenly you too are a kind of Black or Jew or leper. In any case you're in some way pushed into the position of an outcast.

For me it was clear from the outset: I liked long hair—with the long hair you start getting a different relationship to yourself—a new identity—at least, that's how it went with me. You develop this really healthy narcissism which you need simply to survive. After the initial confusion, you become more conscious and start to like yourself.

When we lived in Berlin, I grew up in one of those shitty working-class suburbs. You were really isolated there, and there weren't many people you could hang out with. It was a real achievement to be able to last through the thing. You always had complications, even with other young people. The conformists broke off contact with you, of course—they didn't want to be thrown in the same pot with a bum like you, or they got hassles at home—you know how it is.

So you start building contact with a few people like yourself, other dropouts, or whatever you want to call them. You begin to orient yourself differently.

I never looked at books before, because no one encouraged me to—at most, Karl May or Jerry Cotton*, crap like that. Then I started to read Allen Ginsberg, Jack Kerouac and Sartre, Jack London too—I mean, people who had gone through similar things. These were the influences you picked up when you started getting away from home.

The first day of my apprenticeship, on the ride to the construction site, it suddenly hit me: you're gonna be doing this for fifty years, there's no escaping it. The scare of that just stuck in my bones. I had to look for ways to get out.

Even in East Berlin I had been an outsider because I wasn't in the Pioneers.** At home I was surrounded by women—I was

*German writers of American-style Western novels.
**Soviet Boy Scouts.

conscious of always having to hold onto myself, to always press myself against the dominant current. So it came easy to me to 'drop out,' to go along with this thing—it was the first time that I wasn't the isolated rebel, I found a certain philosophical direction in it, if you know what I mean.

You can only explain and analyze many of your actions after they've happened. You recognize your earlier intuitive rebellions as completely appropriate correct behaviour in the face of some bourgeois dimwit.

The Movement begins in Europe in '64 and '65, gets bigger, steps out more, is recognized for the first time as a phenomenon, and is taken up by the media. In those years the actual breakthrough of all this stuff about the 'post-war generation' gets started. Before that, there were these isolated pockets of people. Then it reached the point where it got the larger framework, here in Germany, anyway. There had always been figures like Pedro or Boras* —you know, the archetypes, the grandfathers of the movement, who have always hung out on the street and bummed around. Because of our age we are the second wave. Maybe our political awareness was a little lower, but for those who got into it, it was first of all new, and for the first time it attracted large numbers. This phenomenon, along with the music, clothes, the hair—all the externals—made for a broader framework—the early isolation trip was broken through.

Before the movement consisted exclusively of bohemians. In 65, for the first time, ordinary people participated. The bohemian trip—the pseudo-artists—is always an elitist affair. That is, they feel superior to everyone else in the world, having already put down the bourgeoisie. Of course, there were already scurrilous rituals and symbols, like the army parkas with writing on them, signs saying 'Ban The Bomb,' slogans or names of rock groups, blues people, and so on. This was the time that the Easter March Movement** got going.

That's how I slowly got contact with the political scene, it was a developmental process. It's like this, you constantly draw more opposition because of your perspective against the

*Archetypal German bohemians.
**The first organized German demonstrations against the Vietnam War.

bourgeois world. Then it gets political, for example, with Springer's tabloids*—they were always against us, nobody could stand that pig Springer because he was the biggest instigator. Like after that Rolling Stones concert in the Waldbuehne, where everything was smashed up; that's where it got started, when things were made purposely hard for us. The political content came as a result of that confrontation and the Viet Nam demonstrations. I was there for those too.

At the time of the Gedächtniskirche and before, I still lived at home. Most of the others did too. So your day went more or less like every other normal worker's. You get up in the morning, everybody gets up, the whole family goes to work, father, mother and so on, then you run to the bus stop, and of course you're still totally out of it—I mean early in the morning I'm always totally spaced out. Then you sit in one of these buses; most of the time you haven't even had breakfast, and you have no money for cigarettes, everybody else is smoking, so you're already pissed off.

Then they take you to the site. The city has always bothered me because I grew up in the country—those heaps of factories give me a pain in the ass. So you sit there in the bus, and you hear the same conversations, see the same drawn faces, one drunk always more fucked up than the next. Or you hear about the same shitty TV movie which you unfortunately saw the night before, and then on the bus the next day you get it all over again, horrifying, a thousand interpretations of that shit. Unrested, hungry, you get to work, and as an apprentice you're just Mr. Asshole there too. You can't see any sense in it, you aren't interested in learning any kind of craft anymore. It just breeds contempt in you, you want to tear it down.

I looked for construction work because I thought, at least there you're out in the fresh air. I mean, a factory, that would have been the ultimate horror. As a carpenter, at least you still work with wood, somehow it can be bearable, but nowadays, with pre-fab construction, even that gets to be more and more a screw-driver operation, like in the factory. There's no craftmanship involved anymore.

---

*Axel Springer is Germany's largest newspaper and magazine publisher, a long-time supporter of the Christian Democratic Union. His publications, particularly *Bild-Zeitung,* have run a consistent campaign against the New Left and the counterculture.

For example, I worked under a journeyman, an old East Prussian finishing carpenter who knew stuff that nobody else in the whole company knew anymore—all those roof constructions, half-timbered constructions, you had to have very special abilities in your hands—so that the beams would fit right into each other, so that the weight distribution holds. The old guy knew all this, and he still got off on his work, he perceived himself as a craftsman who could build a house with his hands. To him what was important is that people have a roof over their heads. That work fulfilled him, he had a whole other sense of his life. That old man had something on me. That's how I see it today. At that time I thought he was an idiot, killing himself working there, a pure fool, putting so much effort into that garbage. But you could see that he still found meaning in what he was doing. None of the others did; they reduced everything to piece work—just in it for the money.

In your work, you reach a certain measure of freedom; when you're really working, you recognize yourself in your work, that's exactly what a craftsman does. It has nothing to do with art, it's nonsense to raise it to the level of art. Craftsmanship is the ability to create something with your hands that has a purpose and in some way looks good.

Then I thought: 'Do you want to participate in this mindless activity just to get your old age pension or social security? That's insanity. I'm alive right now, I am young right now, worry about that later. After all, I have a job, I can get by on that, and I always see to it that I have some fun. I mean, I've always preferred running after a girl over running after work, naturally, you get more out of it, and she does too!'

The whole story of the Gedächtniskirche,* with which everything began, was purely proletarian. A worker definitely has more of a relation with rock music than an intellectual does. With you, it's more physical, you're only tuned into the body, not into the mind, and dancing and stuff like that is more your thing, because somehow you're closer to the earth. I mean, it's more a matter of pure feeling with this kind of music. The whole message in rock is fucking or whatever you want to call it, screwing...make love, not war. It's easier for a worker to grasp or relate to that.

*The Gedächtniskirche is a church in Berlin that was bombed in World War I and became a post-war symbol. In the '60's hippies congregated on the steps of the bombed-out edifice which became a symbol of the counterculture.

For instance, I can remember when I wasn't going out in the evenings I used to always lie in bed listening to Radio Luxembourg or A.F.N.*, until late at night. When I heard Chubby Checker's 'Let's Twist Again' for the first time, I got up out of bed and danced the twist exactly as I saw it done later. I had intuitively understood what the guy was trying to get across. For instance, in Cleaver's *Soul on Ice*, in the chapter 'Convalescence,' it's expressed really well, he's right on. I had experienced it quite spontaneously, had the feeling, I mean.

That kind of music isn't a Beethoven trip, no head trip, but purely a body trip. Of course, it grew out of the blues, the cotton-pickers, who simply changed the grind they were forced into all day long into joy, to get the best out it. Well that's how it was with the music, and through that kind of music, such things really affected proletarian circles more than intellectual ones.

At that time, you didn't have your own apartment. Most of us were still living at home and were pretty young, and simply didn't have the money to get our own places.

You just never had a fucking buck. You made sure you had the cover charge to some beat joint and enough for a glass of red wine. At that time there was a lot of drinking. There wasn't really any dope in '65, nobody really knew about it—at best a couple of happy pills, captagon, or some sort of speed. And we hauled out the same repertoire of hard luck stories. There wasn't any big alternative.

You still didn't feel like part of the left; but everything that was in opposition was good, including the neo-Nazis. But there was no swastika romanticism, not that—nobody considered Hitler good, because he was against long hair too. Fascism as such was in opposition though, and you found pure opposition better than this petit-bourgeois mediocrity. You considered everything good that didn't agree with it.

For a lot of people, things became political later, because of the Vietnam business, and the demonstrations that grew out of it. Everything came together with the demonstrations. Our guys were always there—it was a real thing of the street, and everybody got turned on to it immediately. At first it was all fun: you recognized your friends from the Fat Host.

*Armed Forces Network, a radio station specializing in rock and roll music.

CHAPTER TWO

It Becomes Political—1966-'68

The jump from the Gedächtniskirche into S.D.S. [Socialist German Students] happened suddenly for me. I thought my intellectual potentials hadn't been used, and I wanted to develop them, so I went to an evening course in 1966. There were people there who had been on the political scene for a while; they were more into the drive of it. I was more into the music scene, other things—what's called hippy today, or the counterculture—not directly political. The cultural side interested me more because it was the area of life I felt most involved in.

In the beginning of '67 I joined the S.D.S. The people I liked there were of course the people from K.1 [the first commune in West Berlin]. Somehow they were closest to me. The realm of the students, those bookworms—I could never really get close to it, it just wasn't my world.

The K.1 types were more approachable. They were the only ones that listened to the music and had long hair, in contrast to those from S.D.S. who were all straight. K.1. was exactly the right thing; it presented an alternative to the S.D.S. line that there's gonna be a revolution *sometime*, but it's not going to change anything in your situation right now.

For me, K.1. was the right connection of politics and counter-culture; it was somehow a good combination. It was political—people had a political idea, or knowledge; and they had a style of life, a concrete alternative, this collective living.

Some concepts were totally new to me: the possibility of changing yourself, your lifestyle or your identity. These possibilities didn't exist in Bohemian circles, where everyone had his narcissism, or played out his own fantasy. There were many of those who got stuck along the road, they kept pouring Vermouth into themselves. There are still some of them around today who tell the same stories they told ten years ago, they still look exactly the same, and still sit in the same way in front of the Gedachtniskirche.

What it's about is getting yourself into a new life process, so that you discover this ability to develop at the same time. This was an important point at K.1— that through collective living your relationships to people are changed. I just checked it out and discovered a whole lot of new things, even though at the beginning I didn't really understand in detail what they were saying. Reich theories, monogamy, and so on. With us, all that had been simple: sometimes you slept with a chick*, then with another one, you were constantly chasing them, and at that time so many of them were chasing you, you never worried about a thing. If you had long hair, there was always an incredible number of chicks hanging onto you, all these factory girls. They thought it was great, a guy like that, who had some kind of presence. Straight types were really out of it then. It was a really good time, much better than today. So that stuff didn't interest me too much at the time, they were bourgeois problems, and didn't really exist for me—all these psychodramas being played out in these circles. Love affairs always ran heavy, so Reich, the sexual revolution, all those things did interest me in a way. At that time I also learned a lot from Rainer [Langhans]. He was the psychospecialist in that area. I found it all very good, and very complex, this K.1.

K.1 was a kind of centre. All sorts of characters showed up there, and it became a kind of institution. But the euphoria disappeared quickly. These guys started out and thought about communal living, and made that more and more their thing. But it took over a year before more such living places came into being. For a long time, they were isolated. It was like the situation with the Bolsheviks in Russia. At that time too, it didn't turn immediately into a world revolution; therefore they had to hold back because the pressure from outside became increasingly greater. For K.1 the pressure came as a result of our actions, the courts and so on, and because the experiment was happening only in one house. And there were too many people

*Bommi uses the German word for 'bride.' It carries much of the sexist implications of 'chick' or 'broad,' and fell out of use after the German women's movement grew.

going through there all the time, the membership was always changing. The model didn't unfold properly because something like this can only unfold when several such models come into being and communication begins among the individual cells. That's how K.1 was conceived of: that this style of life would spread, that the process would become more complex—not just a discovery of revolutionary ideas from books, but something that gets immediately translated into action at every point: even in the areas in which things are most destroyed among us Europeans— sexuality, the relationships people have with each other. But K.1 remained a single unit for too long, and fell apart as a result of it. There was K.2, but that was a purely political commune.

Because I grew up in the East, my relationship to Marxist ideas was somewhat disturbed. I experienced the disaster on a practical plane. My first political book was Che Guevera's *Guerilla Warfare*, and then the biographies of anarchist bombers. Generally, anarchist stuff was what I read first, and stuff like the *Communist Manifesto*, and other such things. Violence was a perfectly adequate means, I've never had any hang-ups about it.

Even in K.1 in '67, I was always in favor of building bombs. I really liked Roy Clark,* the bomber who blackmailed the railroad. I wanted to make a leaflet about him in K.1, to show that he was one of us, that he should come and help us, that he's all right—he had found an area of praxis. But the others were opposed to it.

At any rate, it was clear to me that revolution is a matter of violence, and at some point you have to start with it, so you prepare yourself for it as early as possible. The tendency was always in that direction: if you're going to do a thing like that, then do it right, take steps in that direction so that one day you can effectively use this violence against the apparatus. The apparatus showed itself very quickly at these actions: police truncheons, arrests, court cases (Fritz Teufel), house searches, and whatever else there was at that time. Violence in the political realm was never a problem for me.

The students at that time had a lot of difficulty defending themselves against the pigs, simply because of their upbringing.

---

*Roy Clark became a kind of folk hero to people in the counterculture, much as Marion Delgado, the boy who derailed a train by putting a coin on the track, was a hero to the Weathermen in America.

I didn't have those problems; I always hit back if they tried to grab me. That's why I was never arrested at a demonstration.

Everyday in K.1 the newspapers were picked up by 10:00 am., breakfast was ready, and everyone sat around the breakfast table. Each of us read a paper with a pen and scissors, and all articles were cut out and pasted in the archives. Every day we added to the archives, and everyone worked two or three hours on it. The archive in K.1 was an important component of our trip with the press.

First, stories were cut out which had anything to do with us, communards hassling a mayor, or throwing a bucket of paint at a university professor, or making statements about free sexuality—these things were all cut out, and the pictures with them. As well, everything about politics, criminality, scientific stuff, drugs, music; in other words it was an archive for every theme.

There was a great interest in the press. We figured out particularly how the press in Berlin would react to an action, how they would interpret the thing, and our strategy was planned with that in mind. There's a mistake in that, because the position of the bourgeoisie toward revolutionary action is clear in the final analysis; one should not measure one's actions against it. There's far too much attention paid to the media, which lies in capitalist hands. There was a general tendency to overestimate the media, which later had unexpected effects. With K.1 it stayed pretty well within limits, because our point was to bring the idea of the commune to the world.

In the course of the day, disregarding dishwashing and cleaning up (it's clear that's not worth talking about), there were always people over to visit, and we talked with them, or went out to take care of things. We did a lot of pirate printing at K.1, in fact we put that idea on the road. Here too, the archives could be used—used to create new media. The whole *Steal Me Book** was collected out of things in the archive.

At that time, Antje was the only chick in K.1. There was a problem there that K.1 was forever chewing on. These guys were still somehow uptight, they just couldn't get it together with the chicks, because they always built up some kind of expectation around it. They couldn't simply say, 'Hi there.' There was

*Published by Voltaire Press, West Berlin, 1968.

always an incredible number of schoolgirls who came over, of course, they thought we were far out. So the guys said, 'That's our fan club,' and that's the way it went in K.1; or they would send them out to run errands, and already it was just like it is with apprentices. It's that same old story again.

Then sometime during the day, there were discussions in which the specific behaviour of one of us would be examined—his demeanor and his reactions toward a specific thing. There was an important thing in that. It wasn't always friendly and in solidarity—sometimes it was compulsive. For example, these court appearances. When they were going on, there was always a tendency in these discussions to say, 'you didn't raise enough hell.' Already there was pressure to achieve.

Somehow it was all the same to me, because for me this was essentially an apprenticeship. If someone explained to me that I had done something wrong, I told them how I had seen it at the moment, and that was it. I never gave such things a great deal of significance. It was part of it all, so it was okay. At times it could take on a regular sado-masochistic character, this eternal self-criticism and complaint against the others. I never got involved in that trip myself, and I don't see that anything changes as a result of it. Your conditions can only change concretely if you translate them into action, and not through some psychoanalytic discussion. Sometimes the whole thing made me sick, this digging down, because in the final analysis it did nothing.

It was always good when we were planning actions, it was a real up. When they went well there was always great joy in the house. There were always little jokes in them, they were fun, there was laughter in them. There was real craftsmanship too, so that things were put in their appropriate perspective, so that their symbolic value would come out. And it was always great, when things went well, when you came home and saw it on the evening news. It was always fine.

Fritz [Teufel] was released from jail once for a short time and had to report back, but he never did—he was hidden. Then we announced that he would report again at a certain time, at city hall. He was going to put himself there and produce a so-called be-in. K.1 got the first be-ins going. So we wanted to bring the thing to City Hall and to the heads of the city, the parliament, and lay it out on the table for them, and ask them how they related to the case, so the justice machine wouldn't just run its course, completely anonymously. So Fritz shaved off his beard; from the pictures everyone knew him with a beard, Teufel was a concept with a beard, and then he appeared there clean-shaven, with a suit, without glasses, with his hair cut, handing out leaflets saying 'Freedom for Teufel'. Then we stormed the parliamentary hall, and some of us sat down and shouted, 'we want to talk about this case here with you!' But they threw us out again, and finally Fritz was recognized by one of the pigs down in front of city hall and arrested. So we moved to police headquarters and occupied that too, and there I got beaten up by a pig, and they chased us away.

When I got into K.1 Peter Urbach* was already there; he was a marginal figure there. He didn't sleep there, naturally—Urbach always lived at home with his wife and children and mother-in-law. He was an orphan. He was a perfect spy, a good agent. With his orphanage stories he could always endear himself to anyone he wanted something from. He had always conducted himself that way, in the orphanage and with the counsellors. And he could unlock your psyche. That had been his learning process, and he could use it to find out anything he wanted to know. Because he was always friendly and helpful, and seemed completely trustworthy in his relationships, things didn't become very noticeable. Occasionally he was invited to move into K.1 with his wife, but in its way K.1 was an elite bunch too; they never really figured the guy out. For me it was simply like this: if the guy is there all the time, he must be all right. At that time no one had really thought yet about the problem of the infiltrator. The great thing was precisely that you could communicate with everybody. So then you come up with an infiltrator. In bourgeois society, the problem presents itself a little differently. Someone like a tattletale in school, or someone at the construction site that always goes to the foreman, is always recognizable because he conducts himself in a different manner.

The story of the slashed tires was around '68. I did that more or less alone. A lot of aggression got released in a totally

*Peter Urbach was heavily involved in the K.1 scene, and was later found to be a police agent.

irrational action. I was living in one those developments where a
lot of cops live. Where you can see that cars are more important
than places for children to play. My whole disgust toward these
object relationships just went through me one day, and I started
slashing tires, I did them in to the tune of about a hundred. In
other words, I slashed the tires of about a hundred cars with a
knife, a kind of stiletto. *'Walk!'* Even the Herr Reverend's car.
There was some kind of a church around there too.

Most of the cars were in front of this highrise where the cops
lived. That made it more real. Of course, in the papers it was
made to sound even more irrational. But somehow, the action
wasn't bad for my later development; one could reflect on it, it
was simply one of those 'go get 'em' things that have to happen.
You have to see that people can be driven so far that they can
only free themselves by irrational aggressive actions.

It was all more or less spontaneous, not something you talk
about beforehand. I was just sort of wandering through the
area, a little drunk.

When you stick a stiletto in a tire, it is immediately
damaged—slashed from side to side, not on the profile: they go
zip and deflate. I did that with all four of them. It was crazy
work. That's why they caught me. Someone saw it, so they
grabbed me. I got nine months in the joint, and had to pay
damages. It was 3 or 4 thousand Marks.

I had to sit out the whole nine months, I couldn't get around
it. They struck my probation immediately. The prosecutor was
Boehmann, who does all the political trials today. The judge
said, 'If you had slashed all the tires in front of the Wannsee*, it
would have been much better.'

The comrades, of course, all found the action ridiculous—
even K.1. Then an open letter to me appeared in the
Linkeck**—they had simply accepted the story as the papers had
written it up. It stuck to me for a long time. It was a kind of
dropping out for me, more or less, completely uncontrolled.

The tire-stabbing happened at the same time as the
department store arson in Frankfurt† and a K.1 position paper

*A wealthy district in Berlin.
**Berlin underground paper.
†April 1968.

appeared in *Der Spiegel* denouncing it. But I naturally put myself on the side of Baader, Ensslin, Proll and Soehnlein, who had set the fire. That was a much better thing than mine. I didn't denounce it; I considered it good. But the others, Rainer and Kunzel [Dieter Kunzelmann], denounced it. They said it was just psychological failure, that these people wanted to go to the joint*. In that sense, it isn't political anymore, because they acted like such dilettantes that they were immediately arrested. It was precisely this 'psychological failure' that evoked solidarity in me, sympathy, actually—rather than the action itself. I didn't give a shit at that moment whether they actually set a department store on fire or not, just that people broke out of their limits for once and did something—even if they acted in such a way that they were caught. It was precisely here that everyone should have stood behind them in solidarity, and said, 'it's clear, they're all right, they belong to us.'

The split was starting, with the whole left saying 'we have nothing to do with them'—it was the same business over and over, just like Easter of '68. It was said again, we can't frighten anyone, we're distancing ourselves from that, we have nothing to do with arson.

Of course, the arson was a matter of competition too; an attempt to claim a vanguard position through practise. 'The vanguard creates itself'—Che Guevera. Whoever does the heaviest action determines the direction.

There was the general accusation, 'you're too soft,' and so on. When there were court actions at K.1, someone always said later: 'you could have done more, you held back here.' Somehow it had an infantile streak; I knew stuff like that from school. The irrational pressure to achieve was brought in, which in the final analysis remains abstract, because it's a matter of self-assertion, and it makes the thing increasingly serious and humorless. That's why the action form of 'happenings' failed: not only because of the opposition, but also because of internal pressure to achieve. So the individual's capacity to achieve was overridden, manoeuvering one further and further into situations in which you didn't know beforehand if you could make it through.

At the end, everyone in K.1 had endless months of time to do:

*Common term used by prisoners and political people to refer to prisons.

me because of the tires, the people in Frankfurt, of course—you have to see all this as a closed group now—others for disturbing the peace, insulting cops, here this and there that. It kept adding up, until suddenly out of nowhere, for some little prank, the question of being illegal posed itself sometime in '69.

Rainer got pretty scared when he had to sit a year. He couldn't see clearly what was coming down on him anymore—and Rainer had been one of those who had created the pressure to achieve. Somewhere in the process, he just surpassed himself, in all that running around.

I can see it like this because of that business with the tires. That was a situation in which I was pretty down. This demonic circle kept catching up with me: going to work and, in the background, my parents' home. It all kept coming at me because I wasn't really rooted, and didn't know what I wanted. Of course, there's a possibility that you can make one of those truly radical breaks at a time like that, and consciously put yourself outside, blow all the limits, and then you can see further. But of course, you can only decide that for yourself. That's the difference: to say you *should* have done more in court is nonsense, but if you stake it out for yourself beforehand, and see that you still have that much energy, *then* do it.

Every slave waits only for the moment the overseer lets his whip fall—in order to strangle him with his chains, if he still has strength enough and pride within himself. The power of the powerless receives its clear expression in spontaneous action, but that really is an individual thing. That is how the individual terror of the old anarchists can be explained.

You make the revolution for yourself, too. It has to contain all the facets necessary for you to unfold within it and somehow get on the right road, so that this petit-bourgeois nonsense doesn't keep throwing you back; the more radically you break out, the better. Customary mechanisms that act upon you are much stronger than an exceptional situation you create for yourself through some action. With that you get clear more easily, because at some point you determine the conduct. It isn't being done *to* you; instead, you're influencing it. So then the question is whether you have correctly judged your strength—which is also self-recognition.

Then there is the propaganda of the deed, which is something else again—here you decide for yourself too, but inside the framework of a mass, very concretely, in a street massacre. There you build propaganda by standing somewhere in the front row throwing rocks at the porkers. Your conduct within that framework has a different effect than night and fog actions, which become known through the media—in that case the decision is much more an individual one. In one of these street massacres, it's propaganda of the deed: there you don't do it as an individual. A couple of people get together and throw rocks, and simply don't let the bulls get close. Strength is demonstrated for the others, and then they participate. They show that we're not just slaughter animals always getting the club over our heads; we can defend ourselves, it's possible, it's a different relationship—there are many different facets to it.

At the time of the attempt on Rudi Dutschke * I was completely immersed in the political scene and saw myself as a political activist, very consciously, and considered revolution an alternative, as in Cuba or China, or even the events in Kronstadt. Russia and East Germany meant less and less to me at that time. I knew all that. Since '65 I had read a lot, and liked it— I always had a book with me to read during breaks at work, and on and on the bus. But I didn't read any Springer papers.

I left K.1 and went back to work. Sometimes I lived at home. And there were always other places that the dope people had going. Through the Living Theatre†, drugs had come into Berlin by then.

Because I had access to various scenes, the political scene as much as the dope scene, I could move in broad circles: in a section like the Maerkisch Quarter as much as in the workers taverns. It was actually quite a good thing. Sometimes I lived in one of the pads in the Kreuzberg,** or joined in with a beat music band, played harmonica, sang out of tune, simply had fun. I always worked at construction sites as a paver, or cement worker.

*Rudi Dutschke was the best-known spokesman of the German New Left, much like Daniel Cohn-Bendit in France, or Abbie Hoffman, etc, in the U.S.
**One of the most delapidated residential districts in Berlin. It became a kind of Haight-Ashbury.
†Experimental American Theatre troupe.

At Easter, I had known Rudi from S.D.S. and just about everywhere. Rudi was different from the students. I was often with him at the university cafeteria, where we'd sit around at a table—it was cheaper than anywhere else—and shoot the breeze, or later, watch his child. I always had a good relationship with Rudi. He was a really amazing guy.

Rudi's talks were pretty abstract, and not everyone understood him—at least, I didn't—but if you just talked to him, he was a perfectly normal human being, natural, just like everyone else; and really, that's the most important thing. But he had the power—you could see it right away: that man was no bookworm or rhetoric spouter, he was really on top of his thing. If you saw him upstairs in the S.D.S. office, in his apartment, he always cleaned up and took care of things. With that guy you knew that he wouldn't lie to you.

That's an important thing, too: it's why a lot of workers didn't get involved with the student movement. Instinctively you see that that's actually the guy at the top who you're always having trouble with. It's that healthy mistrust. And that mistrust is still rooted—it's actually the last bit of class consciousness that's still intact in the workers. That they didn't get involved in this student thing, in this A.P.O. number, is really a question of class consciousness.

The German working class has been sold out by everybody, be they socialists or mad Hitler. Everyone came and just shit on them, all the way through, from red to black, from Communists to Nazis. It just didn't happen like this in any country like it did in Germany, so there's good reason why they're not getting involved anymore.

But with Rudi, a guy like that, you noticed right away, he's all right, he'll go through fire with you. He won't just split when things get heavy. With the other students, I checked the thing out for myself, emotionally: 'how will he act in another situation?'

Today when I think about how I saw people, emotionally or instinctively, everything is verified. There was a certain kind of arrogance with many of these students. So the mistrust was justified. I just listened at first, and checked it out, because first of all, I had to think myself into these things, into these processes. I never had much to say there.

I dropped from my circle into this thing all by myself. Not very many took part in the political trip: I was pretty much the first one from our group to get into it. I took leaflets with me to work, or Mao Bibles, or 'Disenfranchise Springer' notices, or the *Extrablatt**. Everywhere I went, I gave out leaflets. I gave books to friends I still knew from school. So I tried to agitate in the circles I could reach. Of course, I had good access to these people, because they knew me beforehand, either as a co-worker or a school-friend, and they knew that I was one of them. I could always talk to them and they had to talk to me simply because they worked with me or some such thing. They often read Mao too. But then you'd change jobs, and wouldn't know what became of these people.

*Berlin underground paper.

---

50 „Ordner" pro Demonstrant

Studenten-Kabarett unter dem Funkturm

50 MARSHALS PER DEMONSTRATOR
Student Cabaret Under The Radio Tower

One can demonstrate against a prohibition to demonstrate, too. Peacefully and with humour, approximately 4000 students carried their signs saying 'Albertz Step Back'* yesterday from the Hammerskjeold Place to the Theodor Heuss Place. The ruler was not designated as a murderer, and was also not insulted as such. The anti-demonstration prohibition demonstration was only given a permit with the proviso that the political

*Heinrich Albertz was a conservative member of the Berlin Senate.

heads of Berlin would not be insulted, and that the grass at the Theodor Heuss Place would not be stepped on, and that there would be one marshal for every fifty demonstrators.

The students asked themselves, demonstrate through us today [*sic*], and had leaflets saying 'What does the Senate want to find as an answer?' 'Burdening the majority of the population when a minority demonstrates.' the demonstrators were really a minority—one for every fifty marshalls with armbands and fake service numbers. The marshalls carried 'demonstrator' signs and others with polite slogans: 'Heinrich, you make me shudder,' Albertz, Priest? Duensing, Butcher?' and 'Albertz, where is your brother Ohnesorg?'

They were divided into blocks over a loud speaker system. 'Troublemakers' quickly came into the 'realm of student measures,' an expression learned from the police. They too held back a great deal, and 'regulated traffic,' which despite all fears did not come to a stop.

The Berlin Bear is covering his eyes and being ashamed of himself.

Nor did the discussion between passersby and student debaters come to a stop at the Kudamm.* A little old woman was convinced: 'They're all coming from the East and are against freedom.' It did the students no good to assure her that they were demonstrating precisely *for* freedom. Even the 'Communes' proved orderly. 'Radicalinskies of the World, Do Penance' was the motto of their procession in white robes. 'Radicalinskies' who wanted to provoke during the speeches at the Theodor Heuss Place were booed down.

Even when the city councilman Reistock from Charlottenburg polemicized too sharply against the C.D.U., he was booed down.

A new beginning has been made on the part of the students. Mockery did not turn into a riot. This is a hopeful sign for the future.

Reifenstecher gefaßt

„Kommunarde" gestand: Über 100 Fälle

„Ich habe Autoreifen zerstochen, um gegen die Gesellschaft zu protestieren." Das gab der 20jährige Hilfsarbeiter Michael Baumann aus Reinickendorf als Motiv dafür an, daß er in den letzten Wochen in der Umgebung der Holländerstraße über 100 parkende Kraftfahrzeuge beschädigt hatte. Am Oster-Sonntag früh wurde Baumann zusammen mit einem Komplicen auf frischer Tat gefaßt.

Nach seinen eigenen Angaben bezeichnet sich der 2ujahrige Hilfs-arbeiter als Kommunarde, als Angehöriger der Außerparlamentarischen Opposition und als Mitglied des

... IMMER ETWAS BESONDERES
Burger

Republikanischen Clubs. Ein Ausweis dieses Clubs und eine Mao-Bibel wurden bei ihm be-schlagnahmt.

Seinen eirmal im November 19.. ...

Baumann beschäftigen: Damals hatte er aus München ein Paket mit mehreren Kilogramm Leuchtpulver und Zündern an die Mitglieder der Kommune I abgeschickt. Das Paket war von den Beamten beschlag-nahmt worden. Ein zweites Paket mit 15 Kilogramm Leuchtpulver konnte von der Polizei in München noch kurz vor dem Absenden in der Firma abgefangen werden.

Der Komplice des Hilfs-arbeiters, der 21jährige Hans-Werner Sch., sagte aus, er habe Baumann am Sonntag früh kurz zuvor in einem Lokal

Michael Baumann

kennengelernt und bei der Reifenstecherei aus Spaß mit-gemacht. Der von Michael Bau-mann angerichtete Gesamt-schaden beträgt über 600€ Mark. Beide Täter wurden nach der Vernehmung entlas-sen.

Die Polizei fragt: Wer hat Michael Baumann in den letzten Wochen beobachtet, als er sich an parkenden Wagen zu schaffen machte?

Wolfgang Scherz

TIRE SLASHER CAUGHT

Communard confesses: Over 100 Cases

'I slashed car tires to protest against society.' The 20-year old unskilled worker Michael Baumann gave this as his motive for damaging over a

*The Kudamm is the most fashionable square in West Berlin.

hundred parked cars in the last few weeks in the vicinity of Hollander Street. Baumann together with his accomplices was caught early in the morning on Easter Sunday.

According to his own words, the 20-year old unskilled worker described himself as a communard, a member of the Extra-Parliamentary Opposition, and a member of the Republican Club. A membership card and a Mao Bible were confiscated from him.

The police were concerned with Baumann once before in November. At that time he had sent a package from Munich with several kilograms of gunpowder and fuses to members of Commune 1. The package was confiscated by the officers. A second package with 15 kilograms of gunpowder was seized by the police in Munich shortly before it was sent off by the firm.

The accomplice of the unskilled worker, 21-year old Hans Werner Sch., said he had gotten to know Baumann shortly before in a restaurant Sunday morning, and participated in slashing the tires for fun. The total damage done by Michael Baumann was estimated at over 6000 marks. Both offenders were released from custody.

The police are asking who has observed Michael Baumann in the last few weeks while he was working on the parked cars?

CHAPTER THREE

Easter '68

The story had already started with the Shah's visit in June of '67, when Ohnesorg* was shot—a completely harmless man. After that, things were different.

Two days earlier he had been in the *Extrablatt* office making an order, and I happened to be helping out at the sales desk where I saw him briefly. Then three or four days later I was standing beside his casket, and that gave me a really crazy flash. It's hard to describe it: something terrible got started in me. I couldn't get over it, that some idiot comes along and guns down an unarmed man.

I had been in a lot of barroom fights, and even though they were often really tough, you always kept some semblance of fairness. I had even boxed for a while; I had a different, fully clear relationship toward violence. But a thing like this was just straight out murder to me.

Benno Ohnesorg. It did a crazy thing to me. When his casket went by, it just went ding, something got started there.

And the attempt on Rudi: I had come home from work and driven over to K.1. It was Maudi** Thursday, I'd just been paid. It was Easter, so there were a couple of days off and I thought there's a good thing happening now. And then, when I came in, and heard the news, I just refused to believe it.

So we went to the Technical University, and then of course to Springer's on Koch Street. On the way over we smashed all the windows in the America House. On the way over to Koch Street my whole life ran through my mind. All the beatings I'd had, all the things that happen to you that you feel are unjust. Indignation at the attempt on Rudi was so great in Germany that something happened in every city that same night. The air was so full of sympathy that the bulls didn't dare interfere. They acted differently than usual. There were cops who said, look kids, we can really understand you, but don't go at it too heavy. Through all of that chaos, they really spoke to us.

*Benno Ohnesorg was a New Left student who was shot by the police in West Berlin during a demonstration against the Shah of Iran on June 2, 1967.
**Maudi Thursday is the Christian holiday the day before Good Friday.

Then when I ran across the street, and there were all those torches and the constant cry for Rudi Dutschke, it was the embodiment of the whole thing for me. The bullet was just as much against *you*; for the first time, they were really shooting at you. It doesn't make a damn bit of difference who is doing the shooting. Of course it was clear now: *hit them*, no more pardons.

But people didn't participate in it fully; only the front lines were really into it; the rest of the crowd held back, or took the rocks out of your hand from behind.

And then I met my special friend Peter Urbach, who had these precious molotovs with him, and some others who were getting a bit hot. We got the molotovs out of his car and threw them at the Springer trucks. That was really good. On the spot, I really got it, this concept of mass struggle-terrorism; this problem I had been thinking about for so long became clear to me then. The chance for revolutionary movement lies in this: when a determined group is there simultaneously with the masses, supporting them through terror.

Standing there in front of the flames, I realized that this is how you can get somewhere. Then we went around the corner with a couple of Greeks to one of the Junta* offices and smashed that up too.

A lot of crazy shit happened that night; you got energy from it, a real high. Suddenly you had reached something. Of course it was good too because there was a lot of humor, and that turned a lot of people on too. But the barricades were being crossed from our side, and that was simply the right answer. Up to this point they had come with the little police clubs or Mr. Kurass** shot; but now it had started, with people being offed specifically. The general baiting had created a climate in which little pranks wouldn't work anymore. Not when they're going to liquidate you, regardless of what you do. Before I get transported to Auschwitz again, I'd rather shoot first, that's clear now. If the gallows is smiling at you at the end anyway, then you can fight back beforehand.

Since I grew up in the East I had had a communist upbringing.

*Greece was ruled by a military junta during this period.
**The cop who shot Benno Ohnesorg.

So for me, fascism and the concept of Auschwitz has a different meaning. These same people who gassed six million Jews, they harass you because of your hair, and that's been a part of it the whole time. These dishrags have nothing to say to me about how I'm to cut my hair, or whether my heels are to be 9 cms or 1 cm high.

I thought Easter '68 was our great chance, because it was experienced in the same way by everybody, if only because it was Rudi Dutschke. If it had been anyone else, someone unknown, it would of course never have been that way. He was a little like James Dean for the rock generation, an idol with symbolic value. But beyond that, it was spontaneous experience, insanely strong. Had we continued in the same form, other circles would probably have participated, like in May in Paris; more and more would have been attracted.

The reason nothing came of it all lies with the appeasers. There was no follow-through; everyone got onto the bandwagon of the bourgeois press and said, 'if we look too radical, we'll scare someone? The demand was already there to start explaining things to everyone. It was no longer a matter of collective experience. People started making separations in their heads, into the so-called politicized ones and the workers. They didn't see at all that *this here is my thing and I'm doing it*—if they had, things would have been different. That's how a thing gets followers: if there's someone who stands completely behind his thing, he's the one who'll attract people, gather them together.

The left in Germany never caught on to that. They kept falling into the pitfalls of the press. They kept saying, 'don't scare people off' whenever we showed any determination. But it's exactly that determination that would have brought followers. And that mistrust would have vanished too. People would have said, 'those people are going to go through it to the end.' Total solidarity would have shown more to the people than a short uprising followed by collapse into factions again, and battles in the ditches back and forth.

In the first days after that Easter, you could still sense a togetherness. Shortly after that was the first of May and there were fifty thousand or more on the streets, it was a huge unified Mayday demonstration. At that time the A.P.O. still got crowds. Just that little bit had shown that the people were seeing thing differently. We had an advantage then: everything hadn't been put hard and fast into an ideological framework with its rules, dictums, correct lines, and all kinds of dogmas and rituals. It was still an open thing on all sides, and that's where its indestructibility lay. The opposition can never quite put itself into that place.

On the evening after the burning cars, I drove around with Urbach and Fritz in the V.W., along with a crate full of molotovs, and we were wondering what else we could do. We were too late for the factories; it was around 2:00 am, and from 2:00 on there are people in the plants. So then we looked around at what else we could start, but nothing really came to mind. We thought of setting the Opera House on fire, but then went home sort of aimlessly. We still wanted to drive out to Schwanenwerder where Springer had a villa. We wanted to set that on fire too. But then nobody knew exactly where it was.

The problems of terror had become very real. You had to realize that, without preparation, without logistics, without knowledge or experience, it will all remain a fantasy. You won't be able to do anything. But you can see the possibilities: a small determined group can further conflict like that a little more, can throw terrible wrenches into the works. We saw in our aimless driving through town, that it can't continue like that, you have to be more concrete in order to do anything in that direction.

Rudi described this problem in his forward to *Letters to Rudi D.* *, the Voltaire pamphlet. He enters into the problematic of it, and explains it really well: if there's a determined group, what it can do at that moment, what it can hope to accomplish. This problem posed itself very precisely that night. On the parking lot at Springer's we had clear results. And then it ran into the void, the energy, the activity, there's no goal for it. Your prerequisites are different now. You just can't do it spontaneously anymore.

When K.1 moved over to Stefan Street, they got into things we had done in '65, and drugs came with it. So in other words, where I came from is where they wanted to go. But I wanted to go in another direction, in the direction of terrorism. I didn't live with them on Stefan Street.

*A revolutionary pamphlet, published by Voltaire Publishers, Berlin.

Street fighting and arson such as Berlin hasn't known since the end of the war—the response of leftist extremists to the attempt against Rudi Dutschke. Certain streets became a stage for wild terrorism. Serious street fighting broke out in front of the Schoneberg Hotel. The rioters tried to storm the Hotel Rias [location of a radio station]. At times, they completely halted traffic on the Kudamm. 20,000 police have been put on alert. Already, on the eve of Good Friday, major conflicts have taken place in front of the Koch Street home of Axel Springer. The rioters set fire to cars and smashed windows.

CHAPTER FOUR

The Wieland Commune

Then I started living in S.D.S. Different little actions started, somewhere there would be a molotov, something else would happen elsewhere. There were already several people who had got the idea. People were still very dilettantish and the carry-through wasn't quite right, but you could see the tendency. It got started. You weren't there alone, the collective experiences of Easter '68 had pushed things forward.

In a search for more people, a group formed around the Wieland Commune. At the beginning it was still a living collective, with study groups on *Kapital* at the university. Georg von Rauch* lived there. And then a group formed outside and we moved into the house on Wieland. Ten or twenty of us were living there, with three children in eight rooms, and supported ourselves through pirate printing (Bakunin, *Collected Works*) and store rip-offs. Occasionally, since we never had cash, some guy would invite his father over; unfortunately we'd have put together a huge cold buffet beforehand, a table full of caviar, lox, salads and champagne. The old man comes in, sees the spread, and says he can't eat like that every day, and of course, doesn't give us a goddamned buck. We didn't pay for groceries for quite some time, but just drove around from supermarket to supermarket with a big box in the back and ripped off whatever we needed.

It was a newly formed group, so you weren't into something firmly established anymore, with firmly established fronts. But here there was actually a more intense communal experience. Everyone slept in one room, and all this stuff about breaking down sexual hangups happened there. As a result of the pirate printing, you also got a different relationship to your work. You saw that, when work fulfills you, the results are used differently too, the process by which it comes about, and the content of the work is different, it's fun, it's really good. Up to that point my

*Georg Von Rauch was a close friend of Bommi Baumann. He was later shot by the police in West Berlin. (See Chapter 9.)

relationship to work was pretty fucked up. Positive things happened; totally normal, productive relationships were established inside the collective, and it also served the collective need for money. It's a completely compact thing. Isolation is eliminated this way too, everything. We sold pirate printings in a cafeteria at the Free University, or at the Technical U., and in the political bookstores.

From the beginning, we had a theoretical background for terror in the Wieland Commune: the experiences of the last few years—from '66 to '68, developments within the A.P.O. and the student movement, and on the streets. Then Ohnesorg, and Rudi—that tendency of the state apparatus to show that it was determined enough to do anything. We knew that if it was touched anywhere, it would show its fascistic face again.

The analysis of imperialism tells us that the struggle no longer starts primarily in the metropolis, it's no longer a matter of the working class, but that what's needed is a vanguard in the metropolis that declares its solidarity with the liberation movements of the Third World. Since it lives in the head of the monster, it can do the greatest damage there. Even if the masses in the European metropolis don't put themselves on the side of revolution—the working class among us is already privileged and takes part in the exploitation of the Third World. The only possibility for those who build the vanguard here, who take part in the struggle here, is to destroy the infra-structure of imperialism, destroy the apparatus.

That was the lesson of Paris, May '68, when the tanks were going to intervene, and DeGaulle delegated troops stationed in Germany back to Paris because they were the most dependable. At that point, the bridges should have been blown up, so that the trains with the tanks could never have reached Paris, where they could have created another bloodbath like the 1871 Commune.

Books like *Letters to Rudi D.,* which I've mentioned, or Robert Williams' *The Urban Guerrilla,* Debray's *Revolution in the Revolution?*, or Mao's writings, or Che Guevara's speech, 'Make Two, Three, Many Vietnams' made up the literature of the Wieland Commune.

A smaller group within the commune formed itself into the first urban guerrilla cell. Some had already started looking for better stuff than molotovs; that is, bombs. And there was another group in the city that built transmitters, and we used them too.

Our first big action was Nixon's visit. We drove through Berlin with the illegal transmitters, broadcasting. And along the way I planted a bomb, to give Mr. Nixon a little scare. I placed it in such a way that it wouldn't accidentally hurt a passerby. (It was just a beacon.) It couldn't have done much damage to his little tank car either. The thing wasn't that good. It was made with a timing device, and Peter Urbach had once again put that into our hands. The night before we had run into him at the Republican Club at the teach-in for Nixon's visit. He laid this precious time bomb on us in a plastic bag, and I took it with me.

At the same time, the police were handing out leaflets around Berlin saying, 'Be careful—Don't let strangers into your house.' That was their first great 'state-of-emergency' exercise*. And it was the Security Police** who had put the bomb into our hands through Urbach. We couldn't see through that at the time. Unwittingly, we were a very specific element of the bulls' strategy.

There were hardly any people around who could teach us anything technically, so you had to learn everything for yourself. But the form of the action, the organization, that's the most important thing in the whole affair. You learn that through little practice steps. Of course, the Nixon bomb didn't function. Some ignition wire was broken. We hadn't seen that. The next night we picked it up again, and disarmed it. And a few days later there was a house search. They went through the whole place and found nothing. The bombs lay hidden in the kitchen cabinet. At K.1 there was a house search too, and the same kind of bomb was found over there. Urbach had put it there, and Rainer and Dieter were arrested. After that, posters went up saying, 'Free Kunzel and Longhans.' We organized demonstrations in front of Moabit Prison, Easter '69, which turned into more street slaughters. There was one on the Kudamm too. In the meantime, there had been a rise in

*The State of Emergency Laws, passed in June '68, gave the police extensive and extraordinary powers.
**The federal police force, charged with 'the protection of the constitution.'

militance as a result of the slaughter on Tegeler Way on the fourth of November—where, for the first time, everyone proceeded in unity against the violence of the state with violence. Already there was a higher form of militance than at Easter.

The Rockers* were out too; some of them had been in my class, I knew all of them from the Maerkisch Quarter, they were sort of former school friends of mine. They were also frequently at the Commune.

There was progress in terrorism to be seen at this time in the Wieland Commune. It was important that we continue with it. But again difficulties within the group led to the eventual demise of the commune. We—the group who were into terrorism—had advanced to the point of denying demands such as the expansion of communal experience or the destruction of bourgeois relationships. We said, if you've got the correct political praxis, the rest will solve itself. Not only to see the commune as a single form of praxis, but as well to translate the experiences and the energy generated from within the commune to the outside by political praxis. That was simply a continuation of the K.1 experience: it kept getting more and more abstract, until only the nightly psycho-analytic sessions were left, which in the end have no results.

Political practice doesn't have to be terrorism, it can be anything—even daycare, things like that. But we just happened to be active in that area. We saw it as political work inside the total framework. It isn't the whole story, it's just one part—but that was the part we wanted to do. These were the problems, then, that finally led to the demise of the Wieland Commune, even though good experience was gained there. We began to destroy the dilettantism. We began to get arsenals together, and had already made ties. The thing looked different. We had had our first experience with night and fog actions. We had taken the first step, and had begun to get a handle on the dilettantism.

*Street people into Rock-n-Roll.

CHAPTER FIVE

The Hash Rebellion

Drugs were spreading at a terrific pace. At first not many people in Berlin were taking dope, but by '68 it was beginning to attract a wide following.

I'd taken a couple of drags on a joint once before, when there wasn't much around; I had a trip or two; then more and more dope began to be used. There were people around us in the Wieland Commune who said, 'let's take dope and learn to communicate.' They would sit around in a circle and smoke, and say how great we are. But we said, integrate dope into praxis too, no more separate shit, but a total unification around this thing so, that a new person is born out of the struggle. There shouldn't be any more specialization, but an elimination of the division of labor in every part. Just smoking shit ain't gonna get nothing.

This is how many of my buddies around Easter of '68 were in part politicized—people from Gedächtniskirche, or other folks who had taken dope, who always hung around the Wieland Commune.

So a new group was formed and the Hash Rebels came into being. We said, 'no private living quarters anymore. Further the destruction of private property, keep only those things you wear.' And a whole troop of us started wandering through the city. There were enough places to live, so you could always go somewhere and do a guest performance.

It was a good time, that whole summer of '69 until the beginning of '70. For almost a year we moved around through Berlin. All you had was a piece of shit in your pocket and a skeleton key, and a little money and you had some colorful rags on. But nonetheless we were organized in such a way that we could always instigate something.

Of course, there were actions during that time. That's how

883, the underground paper, was formed. We joined in and published articles in it every week.

We gave this loose group a name: "The Central Committee of the Roaming Hash Rebels." We said, 'we do dope, that's an important thing, and we're rebels—sure, we've been that since God knows when.' 'Central Committee' was simply an ironic statement about existing political circles, because that's what they all called themselves. There were a thousand central committees.

Mao provided our theoretical basis: 'On the Mentality of Roaming Bands of Rebels.' From the so-called robber-bands, he and Chu-Teh had created the first cadre of the Red Army. We took our direction from that. We directed our agitation to make the dopers, who were still partly unpolitical, conscious of their situation. What we did was mass work.

The Wieland Commune and K.1's political theory lay in this: that from the so-called lumpenproletariat the first cadre of urban guerrillas would be formed; and we always worked together with them—not to draw back with some group into an apartment, but to consciously take a step toward the outside, to live with those people who were constantly criminalized, who were also in a posture of protest, and conscious of it from a different perspective. There were people among us who had gained their political experience the same way I had. There wasn't such a break between levels and classes; it all fit together very well.

So we began making an analysis and laying out problems and heightening contradictions, where they were concrete for people day by day in confrontation with the police, so that we couldn't say, abstractly, 'now you have to fight as urban guerrillas.'

At the beginning, in the student revolt, things were explained through analysis of imperialism and here we had already translated it into the very concrete conditions of the life of the people. Imperialism has to be fought simultaneously in the metropolis. That was the decisive theory: that there be struggle, particularly guerrilla struggle. And at the same time you have to translate the struggle into concrete conditions. One doesn't fight because there is fighting in Vietnam—you can't expect that from anyone, it's pure nonsense.

We didn't like to see people specifically dealing dope, who just made money from it. But we were dealing ourselves, you have to live off something; we knew countless people we could sell shit to; that was the one thing we had left. You literally lived with and from dope.

It was in taverns like the Zodiak, the Inexplicable Shelter for Travelers, where it began, where we were able to bring it all to a militant level. When the bulls came and tried to raise hell, we gathered everyone outside and tore up the pavement. That was easy to do with the skeleton keys—the revolutionary doesn't need a thousand tools, you just have to become more universal in your application. So you pick up the rocks—somewhere there is a car listening to the police radio—so we'd go for the radio cars and keep them off our necks. Hardly anyone was ever arrested, and they stopped seizing our shit—of course that was the basis of your existence at that time; if you had to keep throwing it away at every corner, you'd go crazy.

Lawyers were scratched up, too, who were always available for trials. Doctors were searched out to help in emergencies, if someone took an overdose, for instance. You couldn't always go to a public hospital.

At the same time, we made an attempt to do some 'release' work; in other words, to get people off their fix, get them unhooked.

We were impressed by the methods used by the Black Panthers in Harlem. We said, 'the passionate fixer can exchange the needle for the gun.' Or: 'if you put down the needle, replace it with a gun in your hand.' Later, the Socialist Patients' Collective (S.P.K.)* in Heidelberg picked that up again. Dr. Huber turned his patients on in this way.

We also demanded free entrance to the taverns and hangouts we were always going to. All work we carried out publically, basing ourselves on the model of the Panthers in Harlem or Berkeley. We put out brochures, or went to pop festivals to hand out leaflets explaining our work and motivations. We also wrote weekly articles in *883*, and held meetings to try to control the dope market, so that no dealer mafia could be created. At that time, the market was still in the hands of the small dealers; the big ones hadn't made it yet. Today, it's the Persian mafia that

---

*A political action group of former mental patients who saw their emotional problems as based in the sickness of society, and their ultimate cure in revolution. Dr. Huber was the psychiatrist instrumental in organizing the group.

deals all the dope in Germany. At that time, it was still the longhairs.

The first dealer mafia got started at the Zodiak. These people said, 'Here, you want to buy a kilo?' and they put a key in your hand for one of the lockers at the Zoo train station. When we got there, it was always empty, of course, not a single gram in it. So we turned their cars over outside the Zodiak and put them on fire, because they'd bought them with money from these phoney deals.

During one of these capers, I was full of mescaline, and people came in and asked, 'Listen, how do we put a car on fire?' So I went to the door and said, 'You just open the gas cap and then turn the car over, and then throw a match into the pool of gasoline.' So they did it. It burned wonderfully. Everyone ran when the police came, except for me—I couldn't move. The flames—do you understand? I just stood there watching it, feeling peaceful and very sure of myself, no cops, no firemen; they didn't even take me as a witness, they just left me alone, standing there.

We also endeared ourselves to the public by doing things like turning over the radar cars that were hunting for speeders. So the bulls ran after us with rifles. They were always waiting on the shore of the Templehof.

And then setting traps: places where the bulls were always pulling raids. One of our girls would call up and say, 'Listen, there's been a burglary at a drug store. Why don't you send a radio car over?' And then these two radio cars would come by and everyone would be standing by the corner with rocks and molotovs, and then: bang! You could hear on the police radio: 'Bertha 3, this is Bertha X. Your car is burning.' Sometimes they shot, too. At Mr. Go's they shot right into the crowd. It just got to be too much for them. This stuff never got into the papers, that they really used weapons. These were the street slaughters that happened every weekend.

Of course, as a tactic, we had it figured that people who were always living in a militant situation would become open to night and fog actions too, so that the connection would be established.

We sponsored the first smoke-ins at the Zoo. Georg did so much dope that he fell over in the bushes.

In the same way, we started to organize get-togethers for all the people who were part of the scene, and then we'd go to Vietnam demonstrations as closed blocs. That was just as much our business. We motivated people politically, and got them out on the street; sometimes we'd appear with three or four hundred people, and we took part in all the Vietnam demos.

A lot of people who took part in these hippy years were precisely those who would take the further step, and actually form the first cadre of urban guerillas. For example, Petra Schelm.* She was there from the beginning, and then later went on to the R.A.F.** She was the first one dead, too. Petra was one of the first to follow through consistently. There was development in that, we really checked out that process. If you're at the peak of your time, you have an overview of history so that you can correctly analyze and kindle such things and such processes. A chance for revolution exists only in this: that you do something out of this consciousness. Just like later, we disrupted the parades of American troops. That became a mass action too, pulled together through *883*. At the end, we had *883* tightly in our fist. We had ten to twelve thousand copies out; it was the biggest German underground newspaper, with the largest weekly edition.

The Central Committee, which of course did not exist de facto, was just a loose group of people: some K.1 people, a couple of Wieland people, and some others who were around the whole time formed the hard core. They always did the militant actions on the street, with whoever would join them. Clearly, that was propaganda of the deed.

We said it's better that we build barricades right away and protect ourselves through our own militance, than spend our nights at Gothaer Street [Police Station] and be hassled. Every time you're down there you get a full dose of the cudgel. All of that was the time of the Hash Rebellion.

From this central core, the name 'Blues' came into being—it later became a name in the Berlin underground. The Blues were actually the Central Committee; all of the colorful types were

*Petra Schelm was a 21-year old hairdresser who joined the R.A.F. and was killed in early 1971 in a shootout with the police.
**Red Army Fraction. The Baader-Meinhof guerillas, avowedly Marxist-Leninist, with a heavy Third World orientation.

part of it, half counter-culture, half political underground. Just 'the Blues,' because we had been through the whole long trip, through the wave of the cultural revolution, we were politicized not so much through politics as through the cultural things which were happening all those years. We had an example in America: M.C.5,* the band; White Panthers in Detroit, the only whites who took part in the ghetto uprisings, and who pushed things forward with their music; John Sinclair and people like that. Later, the Berlin police were looking for hundreds of groups and sects — even hunting a 'terrorist group' called M.C.5!—when all along it was the same crew, who adopted a new name every week. Really good things were happening with names.

But in this climate, there was a tendency among us to simply continue the Hash Rebel trip. There wasn't a strong inclination to really get into urban guerrilla warfare; we were building a group here that will start an action, but the idea was to develop a unity of collective life, and actions that would then arise as a result of that and be placed in a larger framework.

The scene kept getting larger, and it joined with the on-going student movement. We were getting together around Vietnam demos and the like. So there was an intensified moving together, a unified scene could have developed as it did in America, where the total separation between the political scene and the counter-culture wasn't made during those years.

It was at this time that the Marxist-Leninist groups formed, clearly opposed to drugs. They fell into a nostalgia for the twenties. Things like the C.P. under Thaelmann,** a thing that was really finished, had already been proven false. It represented a strong return to bourgeois forms of life.

They said, 'we want nothing to do with these people.' But we were the only group at that time who were militant on the streets, the only form of the movement which was in the process of developing.

A bunch of us went to London for a few months that summer. There we looked at the whole English scene, what was happening there, the release houses too. It was a result of this London business that Release Hamburg later came into being, which was a different program than we had, but was also very good. They rented factories, or occupied them, like the one on Karolinen

*M.C.5 was a 60's rock group from Detroit whose songs had revolutionary lyrics.
**Thaelmann was the head of the Communist Party in Germany in the 1920's.

Street, and established small manufacturing plants in them, where the junkies could find a social base, and survive at the same time. We didn't have that. They opened a macro restaurant, some of them sewed, some formed a film group, things like that. As a result, people had real occupations and real social roots, and the withdrawal went better.

With us, when something was moving, they'd get off junk, but when things started to stagnate, they'd go back on it. All we could offer them was the struggle, and that was irregular.

'Release Hamburg' had much more success in getting people off junk and not letting them sink back into the bourgeoisie. Later they had farms out in the country—anything is better than withdrawal in the city where they just fill you with Valium and put you back on the street, where you'll get hooked again.

Because we were still involved in our legal hassles in the Judicial campaign, we got together the 'Ebracher Joint Week.' The only political prisoner in Germany at the time was Rainhard Wetter, who was sitting in Ebrach because of some demo in Munich. So all kinds of people from various groups around Germany came and held a prison week next to the joint. They demanded that the only political prisoner be freed.

After the prison week, some of our group went to meet the guerrillas in Jordan. They got some training there: how to shoot; how to make bombs; how to fight. They saw the conditions the guerrillas lived in, and explained their own situation. But the Palestinians told them to go back to Germany and make propaganda for them. That was all they were hot for—they never offered weapons.

But after their return, the brothers were saying that the new man—after all, it was always a question of changing man—comes into being with weapons in hand. That's Fanon's phrase: 'As they discovered their humanity, they brought forth their weapons.' That became totally realistic to them. And these people came back from Palestine with that message, and the total will to fight.

During this time the Hash Rebel saga was continuing in Berlin, and the work had already brought results. Every week people got together to discuss problems; the scene had become pretty compact, and was very secure because there were no informers in it. Urbach, for example, was never a part of this. He was still running around and had started to deal shit with a morphine base. So the Secret Police delivered to the junkies; they had a new strategy. It is now known that Urbach really did deal a morphine base. The Secret Police addicted lots of people; the same as in Harlem, where the CIA supplies. It's an old story.

In any case, we had no contact with Urbach—we separated from him and warned people. It was intuition that we couldn't trust the guy anymore, because he had a different lifestyle. There appeared a chain of ambiguities that we just couldn't deal with.

IT IS TIME TO DESTROY.

For some time now in Berlin, the **Central Committee of the Roaming Hash Rebels** has been in existence. The Hash Rebels have announced active struggle against the Police and Administrative terror. They have public smoke-ins, demonstrations in front of withdrawal clinics, revenge hits against the police, legal assistance for persecuted dopers, and have organized a team of doctors for people who have flipped out.

THE HASH REBELS are the militant kernel of Berlin's counter-culture. They fight against the modern monopoly capitalist system of slavery. They are fighting for their own free decisions over their bodies and form of life. JOIN THIS STRUGGLE.

Build militant cadres in towns and cities. Contact similar groups.

Shit on the society of middle age and taboos. Become wild and do beautiful things. Have a joint. Whatever you see that you don't like, destroy.

Dare to struggle, dare to win.

With Anarchist greetings,
Central Committee of the Roaming Hash Rebels

CHANGE YOUR HATRED INTO ENERGY

At a stage in which the movement of the imperialist Amerikan army in Vietnam has become a wild goose chase, the left calls for a worldwide demonstration.

Saturday evening, 11/15/69 is a Vietnam demonstration. A teach-in will take place at the Audi-Max beforehand. What should our solidarity look like? If we have learned anything from the Vietnamese it must and will be seen Saturday evening. Saturday evening we can collectively show our recognition of this bestial society, and unload our frustration.

Saturday evening we will practise the solidarity of struggle with the revolutionary movements of the Third World: Viet Cong, El Fatah, Tupamaros, etc.

The first kernel of urban guerrillas in Western metropolises can only be developed in struggle. Build revolutionary and subversive cells, begin the struggle against the dehumanized system of monopoly capitalism. Create the conditions for a revolutionary people's war here too.

Change your hatred into energy.

Fight on the streets Saturday evening, create massive terror at every street corner the night before. Good targets are American industrial firms, banks, police stations, and everything which makes man into a slave. Show everyone who does not understand it yet that solidarity shows itself in deeds, not just words.

I think the time is right for violent revolution.

The young jokingly throw stones at frogs.

The frogs die seriously.

With Anarchist greetings,
BLACK FRONT

Is 'Hair' the worthy representative of the counter-culture?

No! We even know that *Hair** only appears in the image of the counter-culture in order to satisfy the capitalist's needs. We, Berlin's counter-culture, among other members of the Central Committee of the Roaming Hash Rebels, do not identify ourselves with the *Hair* troupe.

Now as before—before the Senate showed its true colors by closing the Zodiak, the Obdach, etc—the true counter-culture stews underground, outlawed, in illegal apartments.

The appearance of *Hair*, the pseudo-counter-culture troupe, is an attempt to convince the outside that West Berlin, 'The Free City,' has room for everyone!

WE DEMAND THAT THE BEAUTIFUL BALLOON BE GIVEN OVER TO THE TRUE COUNTERCULTURE. IN CASE THIS DOESN'T HAPPEN, WE KNOW HOW TO PREVENT ANY OTHER SHIT FROM CROSSING THE STAGE THERE.

Chase the audience into the street until they scream, yell, and tear down everything that makes man a slave!

Hashish, opium, heroin, for a black West Berlin!

Central Committee of the Roaming Hash Rebels

A HAIL OF STONES FROM THE 'UNERGRUNDLICHEN'

The day before yesterday, on 6/26/69, the shit-pigs led a hunt against us 'criminals and anti-social' elements. They busted 145 of our guys; they held five until today. They vanished, like many of us before, into the

---

*An American smash Broadway hit about the counterculture in the 1960's.

joint at Wittenau and the youth concentration camps. None of us defended ourselves against it.

Yesterday, during the night search, at least a few of us began to defend ourselves. "Last evening approximately seventy young people received two special vehicles of police with a hailstorm of rocks in front of the premises of the Unergrundliches Obdach Fuer Reisende* at the Fasanenplatz in Charlottenburg. Three officers were injured. There was ample damage to the police cars." Actually there were many more of us than seventy, but many of us were standing around stupidly and fucked up on the sidewalks.

IN ORDER TO DEFEND OURSELVES BETTER IN THE FUTURE

IN ORDER TO PRESERVE OUR MEETING PLACES AND GENERALLY GET TO KNOW EACH OTHER BETTER

We will meet Saturday, July 5, 1969, for the

First Berlin Smoke-in
Zoological Gardens

Bring instruments, fabric, records, blankets, tape recorders, and whatever else is fun.

—Central Committee of the Roaming Hash Rebels

Comrades, the situation is serious, we are finding ourselves in a fighting phase in which we are no longer deciding what is to be played, but in which the rhythm is prescribed for us.

For weeks, the police have practised on us what is called robbing people, repression, and arbitrariness.

We find ourselves in the fatal 'You today, me tomorrow' situation. Many good dudes have been arrested under shocking circumstances. They were locked up or simply put into a withdrawal institution, or put under pressure by the most cruel methods. They want to push us onto a dark comfortable sidetrack. They want to isolate us, to demoralize us.

They want to destroy us!

Now it is up to us to get the situation back into our hands. We have to throw those who persecute us into fear and uncertainty.

We have to reach for the most uncalculable and successful methods. Our motto: terror without measure is measurelessly fun—and we will see if we are then treated like wildlife. We have to be clever and thoughtful; we have to surface from the shadows, hit, and vanish again into the shadows.

ONLY WE CAN MAKE OURSELVES FREE AND OH SO HIGH!

With Anarchist greetings,
Central Committee of the Roaming Hash Rebels

We demonstrate our solidarity with our locked up friends
LONG LIVE THE COUNTER-CULTURE

---

* The Unergrundliches Obdach Fuer Reisende was a counter-culture youth hostel.

CHAPTER SIX

Tupamaros* West Berlin

There was a split when people got back from Palestine. The Palestinian faction said, 'things don't make sense the way they're going now. We have to really start with the armed struggle.' That meant giving up the Blues, the whole broad open scene.

A lot of things are left behind, and the armed struggle starts, specifically with the judicial campaign—that is, against the power of the state. The needs of our own people are no longer concretely to be dealt with; this special area concerns only a few, who are already in the power of the courts.

The problem of Palestine is introduced; Vietnam is no longer the ideological framework, Palestine is. Later, in Munich, at the Olympics, one can see to what extent the problem of Palestine is actualized in Germany.

At the time of the amnesty negotiations,** we thought that amnesty either has to brought about for everyone on the left—and not just for individuals—by bombing, so that everyone gets amnesty, and that it be brought about by absolutely massive pressure. Or it can be prevented by bombing—so that they'll say, 'of course we aren't going to give amnesty to these crazies.' This would have the advantage of confronting two or three thousand students right then and there with the question of being illegal or being in the joint. And at that moment it would mean, do we continue or give it up?

Of course, this would give the entire guerrilla movement a tremendous push forward. That was the most important idea to begin with, but it later became an inroad into the apparatus of the state, or an abstract theory of imperialism. With Tupamaros West Berlin (T.W.), as the name indicates, there was another

*The Tupamaros were the world's first spectacular urban guerilla organization. They operated in Uruguay extensively between 1967 and 1972.
**Sentences imposed for crimes commmitted during the Springer and State of Emergency Law demonstrations were not carried out because of the President's amnesty.

factor: the idea that urban guerrilla warfare is possible. These Latin American experiences that were still fresh then had not been properly reflected on; that is, Latin America is (a) Third World, and (b) has completely different metropolises that still naturally contain the general chaos of a Third World city that a settled European capital doesn't have. Because of that, you can still survive there in the most dire circumstances better than you can here in the best of circumstances. Of course, we didn't realize that.

At first, I was in favor of continuing the Hash Rebels. We had constructed some logistics, we'd learned from our mistakes. We had gotten arsenals together with all kinds of stuff, and we still had the receivers and transmitters.

From the moment they got back, the Palestine people had nothing except the will to fight, not a single buck, no place to live in Berlin, absolutely nothing. We were the innermost circle, and had sole access to them. When they returned, they were only available for a few people to talk to. They had short hair, false passports, and were semi-strangers. They looked totally straight; you couldn't go anywhere with them because they looked like informers. Because we were their connection to the base, I finally at some point got involved with a couple of people, because in the final analysis, we naturally wanted the same thing.

Things then got started with the bombing of the Jewish synagogue and the leaflet that went with it, *Shalom and Napalm.*

So there was a bomb planted in a Jewish synagogue, on the anniversary of Crystal Night*. It didn't go off. But everyone flipped out about it, despite the leaflet, which explained the problem of Palestine from the viewpoint of the left, that is, that the new strategy of imperialism centers on Palestine. Since Vietnam is finished, the war more or less over, it can't go on forever; people should get involved with Palestine. It is actually much closer to us, which is apparent today with the oil business, and has more to do with us here in the European cities than does Vietnam. This was to become the new framework to carry on the struggle here. But for the press, of course, it was a prize, because

---

*Crystal Night was the night in 1938 when the Nazis destroyed synagogues, Jewish shops, business and homes throughout Germany.

stupidly enough, it was on Crystal Night, so that Germans had once again set off a bomb in a Jewish synagogue; that wasn't reconcilable anymore.

These people made the mistake of not telling us anything: they would only say, we're going to do an action. Then they explained to us that this bomb was to be the beginning of guerrilla warfare in Germany. Now they had done it. They had started the process. For us, it meant getting on the bandwagon if we were to keep in contact with the spirit of the time, or else just going on as usual. We thought, maybe we can connect it with our things. We can have our thing, and also participate in theirs. We wanted to continue with the Blues, and at the same time support them, and push this process forward once it started rolling.

With the exception of those nine months of probation, I had a clean record. Then we got involved with this legal campaign.

At that time, K. Pawla* was sitting. He had gotten ten months in the joint for taking a shit in front of the judge's bench and wiping his ass with the files. The judge was an old S.S. man; so then we got involved and put a bomb in front of his door. It blew up and destroyed the whole door. These, then, were the beginnings.

Ten or twelve attempts were made against judges, prosecutors, prison superintendents and others. Each time a leaflet went out to the *D.P.A.* [an underground paper] and at the same time a longer one for *883*. And of course each time someone else claimed the action. Overnight, there were twenty groups. This was to suggest that suddenly, overnight, a giant people's army had come into being and was now operating—to create confusion among the police and to show the people that we were already a very large circle. In fact, there were only about ten people or so.

Attempts were made on the America House, the office of El Al, the American officers' clubs, and always there were leaflets to go with them. For communication we had *883* and the illegal transmitters. They weren't strong and could only reach a few car radios. But sometimes the TV would pick us up. We never knew when we were being received. It was crazy—we'd make a tape and drive screaming through the city transmitting wildly. What a gag

*Karl Pawla was a counter-culture revolutionary.

to see Koepke* on the TV news suddenly start 'reading' our guerilla communiques!

We wanted to get the thing out to as large a number as possible, and so always dropped off a leaflet at the *D.P.A.* announcing that this or that group was responsible for the latest action. We were always reproduced word for word, and sometimes the whole leaflet would be printed. But there was already a tendency there to depend on that too much, giving the media too much significance.

The bombs were better now, but nonetheless we had some flops, because we were the Blues. You have to remember that we were terrible Bluesbreakers, we were a crew like the Freak Brothers**. And that was always our problem. It's very comfortable, but very inconvenient for stuff like this. To create a connection between a completely rigid type of thing like that kind of struggle and our expectations for change, which went the route of the Blues mentality, never succeeded, not even at the end.

Things like this would happen: we'd build a totally precise bomb, with all the little connections, and all the little switches and detonators, and then we'd go out at night and arm it at the back of a building, and then drive to the nearest student cafe, beaming with joy, and order a cup of tea. Just starting to drink the tea, we'd remember that we hadn't switched off the safety—the thing won't go off. So drive back, crawl back there, put the switch in place, take one step around the corner of the building—of course we hadn't looked at the clock again, but the hand would be nearly there by then, so we had approximately one second before the explosion—turn the safety switch, take one step around the corner, and everything comes flying after us, all the witnesses staring, and us screaming across the embankment with singed hair, jumping into the car and racing away. So there'd be a thousand descriptions, they look like such and such, long hair, colorfully clothed, everything was clear again.

One way or the other, we were pretty lucky. For example, we were going to strike again, and were standing in front of a window and I had the firebomb. That was a mixture of Pattex and Garbagex, that is, an acid with a combustible mass; it had a sort of napalm effect, because it sticks. Instead of throwing a

*Koepke was a newscaster for the Berlin television station.
**Counterculture comic strip heroes in an American underground comic book series, noted for their bungling and outrageous capers.

rock through the window first, I take the thing and throw it against the plate glass. But the windows are so elastic it comes flying back. I see this little dot of light coming toward me, thank God it was winter, there was snow, and the little dot of light lands right between my legs. I looked down and the thing was slightly burnt, split seconds before the explosion; the snow put out the fuse—otherwise I would have been gone, like a napalm sacrifice. It goes pop, like a giant flashbulb, those things were terrible, we had succeeded in making a horrible mixture. It almost did me in twice, our own invention. These things happened over and over again, with other people too.

The police apparatus began to organize itself—that was a level of confusion no one had counted on, people almost overnight erupting in this way.

Then people in Munich started too, and it looked like it was spreading. There was T.W. as the great signifier—Tupamaros West Berlin, and T.M.—Tupamaros Munich—got involved with the legal campaign, and also made strikes against the legal machine, to show those acting from the desk that they no longer had private lives: 'if you attack us from your desk, we'll catch you at home—you're just as guilty as the jailer, and there's no getting away for him anymore either.' If you make legal decisions like that, you have to know that it's gonna catch up with you at home.

At that time we were still trying to enlarge the framework of the people. We began to rent illegal apartments, had illegal cars, and of course, some of *us* were now illegal too. In the process we made a mistake: we gave two people bombs. At that point very high rewards had been put up, as high as 20,000 Marks, for clues that might expose these actions. The brother of one of these guys must have seen the things under their beds—they lived in some sort of commune too. He goes to the police and says, my brother Berni has things just like that under his bed—the cops always had pictures of the bombs that didn't go off in the newspapers, it was always the same model.

So the search began with that. I was standing in the Park Tavern with a joint in my hand, dancing, when suddenly the lights went on and the cops came in. They are looking at people and have pictures in their hands. I asked one of them what he was looking for, and he says, "None of your damn business.' I looked down at his hand and there was my picture right there. I said, 'Okay, if that's what you think,' and split immediately. The next day, two other guys and I appeared in big print in the press, on the radio and the TV. We were more or less the first ones to have warrants out for us in Germany.

Of course, we were totally unprepared for this—that was dilettantism again; we hadn't included a thing like this in our plans. I had no I.D., nothing. I had jaundice at this time too, had it so bad that I didn't recognize it and I fell over in the street. One of our guys came past and dug me out of the snow and got me into an apartment. Fortunately, he knew a doctor. I had the experience of being dead for two or three minutes—a pretty crazy experience too, difficult to describe. So I recovered from jaundice in an underground apartment.

In the apartment under me lived this bull who watched my parents' apartment during the day. Every morning he went out with the insane hope of meeting me somewhere, and here I was lying right over him with jaundice. I was always going down to use his phone, and had some good talks with the man, and later he even told me what he was doing. He never checked out who he was dealing with.

Later, when I was arrested, he was the first one who came into the cell and saw me lying there. Of course, he was stopped short by the fact that for over a month he had lived with this guy he was searching for every morning in the snow and wind. There was always a laugh somewhere. Work is work, and a drink's a drink.

When we were still legal, we organized the first Hash Rebel teach-in, where all sorts of people made music and talked. I actually wanted to fuck on stage, we always wanted to do these sexual pranks, but by then we couldn't appear too publically anymore.

We sold the exclusive picture rights to the teach-in to a reporter from *Quick* [a sensationalist tabloid]. We handed out Hash Rebel leaflets, and the T.W. faction played another ominous tape calling for armed struggle and all that. But this *Quick* reporter had nothing better to do than look at these bombing attempts, and put everything together in one pot. He wrote a nasty article and spread the worst shit about people.

We decided then that the press could be punished too, that these reporters shouldn't get away unscathed. So we drove over to his place to beat the hell out of him and straighten out the furniture in his house. So we hit him around the head a little and made a mess out of his house, and a neighbor promptly called the cops. They surrounded the place, and smack, we were all arrested.

By that time I was already wanted. It was clear the news was out. That was around February of '70. I sat for a year and a half—at Moabit, and Ploetzensee.*

The whole action was a little crazy, and of course everyone shouted 'say hello to Charles Manson.' When the bulls came in we put on the record, *Sympathy for the Devil*, and yelled 'Hail Satan!' Sure, *Charles Manson,* we wrote that on the wall with red paint. And we were on that trip of signalling with two fingers: 'Hail Satan' was actually our internal greeting. Unconsciously we had touched one of those borderline places—at that time we didn't think Charles Manson so bad. Somehow, we found him quite funny.

We still had a guy among us who celebrated Black Masses in a torn-down house on the Kreuzberg. He turned us on to this. In that film, *Rosemary's Baby*, that's where the 'Hail Satan' is from, at the end, where they're all standing around the crib, screaming.

People like Proudhon, the old anarchists, often were also satanists at the same time; Bakunin too. *God and the State* is actually in some ways a gnostic piece. It has religious content when he says that once we take the Bible seriously, we can only say at the end, 'Hail Satan.' That story fascinated us.

We were also running around at that time, which scared a lot of people off. They called us the Hoppla Brothers** because we were always showing up, hail fellow well met, here I come, sort of à la Hans Albers [popular actor]. Big black hats and black leather jackets, black boots: we were always very dark figures.

---

*Moabit and Ploetzennsee are prisons in Berlin.
**'Hoppla' means 'hullo.' It is used to describe someone tripping in and over things.

Our scarves, of course, were black and red. We never played the *Internationale*, but always Jimi Hendrix.*

We had used the experiences of the Black Panthers as a starting point. So we didn't check out the fact that they had the black community and they could do things like that, they could continue to be guys like this. A man like Cleaver, he's right down our alley. *Soul On Ice.* They were able to make the connection better, because they had the black community, but among us there were only about a hundred men, living somewhere in the Kreuzberg. We never quite realized what that meant, we only had about a hundred scattered through that section of the city, and we had to meet in specific places. But the moment you became illegal you could no longer go to these places because they all knew that's where we hung out.

So we had to figure something out. In '69 there weren't that many people yet with long hair. Because we were known as a group with a very specific style, we had to change on the exterior. So it started with short hair, different clothes, so that we sank to the level of Selbach, a sort of chic boutique.

Then too, the isolation from the Blues group started: you couldn't let yourself be seen as much. Influence wanes as more and more people become illegal, and more and more are taken away for this illegal work, even people who are legal, who had to take care of things. Someone who's illegal has to have a helper who can support him. Three people who were illegal would sit in one apartment, and two or three legal ones would take care of them. First of all, if your picture was on television every day, you didn't go out for a week. So you need someone to get stuff for you, who can do everything for you, because at that time we didn't have any I.D. either.

When I was arrested, the bulls said at my trial that yes, actually I was the most well-dressed, the most polite, the friendliest young man. So already there was a discrepancy—you look different and you act differently. You didn't just show up anymore, somehow you were a little more cool.

*A charismatic black rock star and hero of the 60's counterculture. Hendrix died in 1969 from a drug overdose.

SHALOM & NAPALM*

Four years ago the left movements in the United States and in the European metropolises began to massively demonstrate their solidarity with the anti-imperialist people's liberation struggle of the Vietnamese. Today, shortly before the final and total demise of the Amerikan army, millions of U.S. citizens are demonstrating with the left for an end to the war and thereby for the victory of the liberation front. But the victorious end of the war in Vietnam is the beginning of the Vietnam war on all fronts.

Imperialism attempts to prevent its next decisive defeat by a show of all its force in the Near East.

European and U.S. capital has established a strong military base in the Near East. It actively supports the Zionists in their aggressive expansionist moves into Arab territory. Several thousand U.S. specialists with Vietnam experience are already working as military advisors in the Israeli Army. Over 40% of the Israeli budget is used for so-called defense expenditures. Golda Meir travels throughout the Western world and returns home with Phantoms, dollars, and napalm. The tarnished billions from the B.R.D.,** given as reparation payments and foreign aid, are planned into the Zionist defense budget. After the U.S.A., German investors are the biggest investors in the Israeli economy. Under the guilt-conscious cloak of overcoming the fascist acts of horror against the Jews, it is decidedly helpful in Israel's fascist acts of horror against the Palestinian Arabs.

Israeli prisons in which, according to the testimony of escaped liberation fighters, Gestapo torture methods are used, are filled. Private houses of Arab civilians in the occupied territories and in Israel, who are suspected of sympathizing with the armed resistance, are blown into the air, and the inhabitants chased out or murdered. In rebellious villages where nests of resistance are discovered or suspected, the Israeli occupation army uses terror and revenge measures. Surprise attacks, massacres, and mass arrests are carried on daily. The victims of Israeli napalm bombs lie in Jordanian hospitals.

Once again, the German public knows nothing. Springer lets himself be draped with honorary doctorates in Tel Aviv and builds up Moshe Dayan as a folk hero à la Rommel. The Palestinian people have fought for their independence for over fifty years. The three million Palestinian refugees who have vegetated for more than twenty years in pathetic tent camps have begun their struggle. For ten years they have organized the armed people's war against Amerikan imperialism. Racist and Zionist Israel defends the oil interests of the world police with napalm, phantoms, and German tanks in the whole Arab region. The fascist expansion move of Israel in June showed every Palestinian and every Arab: imperialism can only be fought through lengthy armed revolutionary people's war. The exploited masses in the feudal sheikdoms and the revisionist Arab states no longer expect anything

---

*This leaflet (Shalom and Napalm) accompanied the attempted bombing of a Berlin synagogue in 1969, on the anniversary of the fascist Crystal Night.
**Bundesrepublik Deutschland—Federal Reupublic of Germany-West Germany.

from the radical phrases of their government leaders. The struggle of the El Fatah has shown everyone how imperialism, Zionism, and the system in their own countries is to be fought. The Palestinian revolution is the starting point of all-inclusive change in the Arab world.

On the 31st anniversary of the fascist Crystal Night, several Jewish memorials in West Berlin were sprayed with "Shalom and Napalm" and "El Fath." A fire bomb was placed in the Jewish synagogue. Both actions are not to be defamed as right radical outgrowths, but are a decisive unifying limb of international socialist solidarity. Until now, the failure of the left in dealing with the Middle East conflict with theoretical paralysis is a product of the German consciousness of guilt: "We have gassed the Jews, and now must save the Jews from new genocide." The neurotic historicistic elaboration of the historical disenfranchisement of an Israeli state does not overcome this helpless anti-fascism. True anti-fascism is clear and simple solidarity with the struggling fedayeen. Our solidarity will no longer be satisfied with the verbal, abstract methods of enlightenment a la Vietnam, but will fight the close interweaving of Zionist Israel with the fascist B.R.D. through concrete, unindulgent actions. Every hour of celebration in West Berlin and in the B.R.D. underlines that the Crystal Night of 1938 is repeated daily by the Zionists in the occupied territories, in the refugee camps, and in Israeli prisons. The Jews displaced by fascism have themselves become fascists who want to eradicate the Palestinian people in collaboration with Amerikan capital. Let us destroy the direct support of Israel through German industry and the German government, and thereby prepare for the victory of the Palestinian revolution, and force the renewed overthrow of world imperialism. At the same time we further our struggle against fascism in the mantle of democracy, and begin to build up a revolutionary liberation front in the metropolis.

CARRY THE STRUGGLE FROM THE VILLAGES TO THE METROPOLISES!

ALL POLITICAL POWER COMES FROM THE BARREL OF THE GUN!

BLACK RATS, T.W.

STATION TW

This is Station T.W.
Create Two, Three, Many Vietnams

The trip of the week.

"Operation Uncle Tuca-Tupa" is finished. The comrades have done a good job. The enemy suffered property damage. We made our demands known to the public. All the terrorists who took part in the commando returned to the base undamaged. The result of self-criticism was that traces were left behind in the laboratory, and another comrade was therefore forced to put himself in danger. The comrade suggested as a corrective that a not-to-be-found laboratory be built in West Germany.

"Operation Big Pail" was finished today. The commando succeeded despite heavy surveillance of the house. Technology went by the wayside. The Forensic Laboratory is still in the process of analysis. The results will be transmitted tomorrow to station T.W. Even before the operation was carried out, the explanation was given to the d.p.a. and the bosses of the pig syndicate:

WE DEMAND:

1) Immediate end to the Mahler trial
2) The immediate release of Karl Pawla, Theo Berger, and all Hash Rebels
3) Immediate withdrawal of arrest warrants for Teufel, Kunzelmann, Gebbert, and the Frankfurt arsonists
4) Immediate release of Jansen, Farkasovsky, and Caspari who had nothing to do with the bomb in the Jewish synagogue
5) Immediate amnesty for all political crimes, or no amnesty at all.
   These demands have until now been kept quiet.

A speaker from T.W. gave the following explanation of the Hash Rebels:

We learned with joy that the comrades in the Hash Rebels have learned from the mistakes of the past. Their self-criticism is related to concrete praxis. They could not prevent the RD Pigbull Oehmke from making public speeches—while outside Hash Rebels were being kidnapped by the constables—that Oehmke drove home unharmed and with an undamaged car—and that at the same time the RD Chief Pigbull was also holding public speeches—and that here too nothing was done. Despite intensive agitation, the Hash Rebels did not succeed at tearing the counter-culture out of their mattresses. They therefore decided on the strategy of subversive action. They have begun to organize themselves into small revolutionary cells. Their first actions are in preparation.

Unfortunately, this morning's scheduled school arson was prematurely discovered. The student from T.W. will work in a more disciplined way in all future preparations for actions. As is said by a reliable source, a source for the revolutionary students explained: "There are at least as many schools in Berlin as there are judges and prosecutors, to say nothing of right teachers."

At the end of our program one more announcement:

All persons who live in the houses of judges and prosecutors are now sufficiently warned. Until now, no one has been hurt. However, we bring to your attention that in the future non-participating persons will be putting themselves in danger by their presence in such houses.

OPEN LETTER TO ELEONORE K.
Temporary maid at 46 Leibnitz Street

Your shitty situation, that you have to clean, brings you into the vicinity of criminals like Judge Heinsen.

You are cleaning for a Nazi, for an S.S. Obersturmbann-fuehrer who received the Silver Skullring from his Fuehrer personally, for strangling his own dog with bare hands, for murdering Jews and French resistance fighters as Major of the Gendarmes near Paris. He continues today. He wants to put Horst Mahler through his paces and out of the courtroom. He is allowing Karl Pawla to be handcuffed and brought into the joint. That is enough for us.

These gentlemen exist to destroy us, because we are fighting for our freedom.

All you who are cleaning cannot be neutral. Otherwise, you yourselves will be destroyed. You yourselves must beat and rob these pigs, burn their palaces, fight your oppressors, or you yourselves will be destroyed.

THIS WAS: THE TRIP OF THE WEEK FROM STATION T.W.

Kripo kam um Mitternacht: 20 Festnahmen

Razzia in zwei Hasch-Lokalen

Gestern fünf

Festnahmen

Gesucht wird: „Bär"

Headline: Criminal Police Came at midnight: 20 Arrested; Raid in Two Hash Taverns; 5 Taken into Custody Yesterday.

ARE THESE THE BOMBERS?

Berlin, December 16—The Special Commission of the Political Police yesterday began a massive search for three persons who are under heavy suspicion of having participated extensively in recent bombing attacks. They are 23-year old Bernard Braun, 22-year old Michael Baumann, and a presumed Dutchman who is known by the nickname "Baer."

The massive search by the Berlin Police began with a house search which took place yesterday afternoon in Waidmannslust in the house at Nimrod Street No. 29. Criminal Police supported by a special commando of Security Police surprised and occupied an apartment in the building which was occupied by a commune-like group.

The Criminal Police confiscated a time bomb and a firebomb during the thorough house search. The explosive, according to the analysis of the Technical Crime Research Lab, was of the same sort as the bomb disarmed in the Jewish synagogue and the explosive intended for the attack on the family home of the Chief Prosecutor Savarin in Lichterfelde.

Criminal Police found the confiscated bombs under a bed. Five occupants were subsequently taken along for questioning. The result of the first proceeding of the Special Commission of the Political Police was a massive search started late in the evening for Bernard Braun (Nickname "Happy Dieter"), Michael Baumann ("Bommi"), and the presumed Dutchman known only by the nickname "Baer." "Baer" is approximately 1.78 meters tall, has a full beard, and black hair. He almost constantly wears a pink jean jacket and black jeans.

WANTED: Bernard Braun   **WANTED: Michael Baumann**

QUICK REPORTER ATTACKED

Horst Rieck, Berlin correspondent for the illustrated "Quick," was attacked yesterday in his apartment at 68 Fasanen Street, by three men and one woman. The offenders, who describe themselves as anarchists, beat the 29-year old with a beer bottle, tied him up, and gagged him. Officers from several radio cars took the trespassers into custody. The reporter was delivered to the hospital in Wilmersdorf with head injuries and a concussion, and was released at his own request in the evening.

Among the four taken into custody was the 22-year old Michael Baumann. A warrant for his arrest was issued in December 1969, because he is under heavy suspicion of having taken part in bombing attacks of recent times. The attack on Horst Rieck is presumably in connection with a large photo essay which was published in Berlin in "Quick" in January with the title "All Germany Must Burn," concerning the bombing attacks in Berlin.

Beaten Down and Tied Up

It happened yesterday at 3:30 PM, when the reporter opened his apartment door in response to a ring of his doorbell. Suddenly he saw himself opposite the three men and one woman. He was pushed back into the apartment by them and beaten down with a beer bottle which shattered in the process. Covered with blood, Horst Rieck collapsed. The offenders continued to beat him until he lost consciousness. Then they tied him up and gagged him.

When the trespassers began to search through the room, other occupants of the building noticed the noise and moaning of the reporter. They called the police. With the words "You don't have a warrant," one of the offenders slammed the door in the face of the arriving officers from one of the radio cars. Thereupon the police requested reinforcements and had the firemen called. In the meantime, Horst Rieck succeeded in freeing himself to the extent that he could tear open the door of the apartment. With the words "Thank God you're here!", he let in the police.

Immediately after the arrest, one of the offenders said, "If you say anything, we'll blow your house into the air." At Police Station 131, the arrestees made a loud row. They called to one of the arresting officers, "You have a house, a wife, and a child too."

During their first interrogation, three of the arrestees gave student as their occupation. Only Baumann answered the question with "no occupation." All four will be brought before the magistrate today for suspicion in an attempted robbery.

The police found a sign among the arrestees with the inscription "I am a journalist, and only write garbage." In addition, a spray can with black glossy paint and a brand new link chain were found.

L.R.

An arrest warrant had already been put out against him: Michael Baumann, 22 years old.

CHAPTER SEVEN

Time in the Joint:
February '70—Summer '71

Of course as soon as I got to the joint, a couple of others came in behind me, but after a few weeks they were released. I'm the only one who sits, because of the nine months, and in addition, 'continuing detention pending investigation.' Of course the legal apparatus goes into gear as is the case with everyone today. You get solitary, you don't get visitors, they isolate you totally and start to work you over with all sorts of weakmindedness, and naturally try every legal trick they can get away with, and just don't let you out, because they know, as soon as you're out you'll be back at it again. Exactly the same thing comes into play with the political cases happening now—I experienced all that a year and a half earlier.

Outside, T.W. continues. Until fall of 1970, there is still an attempt to continue the Blues and the existing group. The troop is half legal, half illegal. Everyday there's a hit, but by the end everyone knows who belongs to the group, who it is, and who's doing it. But nothing can be proven anymore: they weren't letting themselves get caught in the act anymore, so that nothing could be pinned on them.

Their cars are being stopped and searched all the time, but people are getting away with it, making hits over and over again. Things like this would happen: someone would be stopped by a radio car, they'd open the door and roll the bomb under the police car, and let themselves be searched. The police car drives away, they get out and get the bomb out of the ditch, and then set it off somewhere. Here again, things got a great push, from Cambodian demonstrations, military parades, etc.

During that time I'm insanely upgraded, as the only political prisoner, ostensible head of T.W. and the Hash Rebels, highly notorious in Berlin. I always was during those years. My poster is everywhere, with every bombing my dumb face was glued to the walls, 'Freedom for Bommi' in every mouth. One poster says, 'Free Bommi,' and underneath: 'Destroy what destroys you.'

That was the solution, the central message: 'Destroy what destroys you!' That was always connected with my name, although I didn't invent the saying, don't even know whose it is.

I wrote letters from the joint to the people outside and some of them were published. That was the role I could play.

Then this thing with Hella started. Actually, Hella was my woman at that time. We were always together; we were a kind of doper couple at the same time. We were together, and Hella participated in this stuff. After I was arrested, she naturally took part in the hits, and was putting up the 'Free Bommi' posters. That was the beginning for Hella.

The problem was, the group was a terrible men's sect. I mean, really, they were just pure oppressors of women; it can't be put any other way, and it's around this that the problem of informers arises. All these senstitivity things which were experienced in the commune and were to result in a new sensibility didn't come through anymore among this troop of bombers. It was eliminated, and then destroyed in favor of rigid actionism. The women just couldn't put up with that anymore.

Hella was a perfectly normal worker. She worked in one of those film copy places. She's Irish, and that becomes part of it too: she had an Irish mentality, sure, she liked to do that kind of stuff. As you can see today, a whole people is getting off on it. She was a year ahead of her people, the typical red-haired Irish woman, actually an insanely beautiful girl. And then she was also doing junk, and was pregnant by me, and then had a miscarriage. And the group at that time did not have the sensibility or the sensitivity to understand a woman in that situation. They were treated like sex objects, and then in an action they were treated like men. That was the only equal rights in the area. They sometimes did more than all these guys together. They were really more daring. Hella, for example, went into the Chamber Court and messed around there for an hour, laid plastic bags full of gasoline into the archives, and then connected the immersion heaters; it's like a time bomb, that kind of thing, the immersion heater eventually burns the plastic and brings the gasoline fumes to an explosion. It was the biggest property damage we had ever done. Nearly the whole Chamber Court burned down, and she did that alone.

At some point, the women just couldn't deal anymore with what was front, what was back, who was friend, who was enemy. Hella was lying in the hospital and had jaundice, and was on withdrawal, and everyone knew she was part of it. Three prosecutors and countless bulls appeared, and worked her over with drugs for 24 hours, and fixed her up with some other things, and just soft-boiled her. They sucked a full confession out of her with torture-like methods. She simply collapsed.

With that, the problem of all informers was posed for the first time: they were people who were pushed into the position of outsiders because of the hardness and lack of sensitivity of the group. They were pushed out, and during an arrest just didn't know anymore who was friend or foe, just couldn't see through it anymore. Especially because their consciousness wasn't that high yet, so that at a certain point they'll just give in. The problem of this kind of informer will surface over and over again.

Hella gave a full confession, she told everything she knew, and that wasn't inconsiderable, that was over three-quarters of a year. Annekatrin*and Hella didn't incriminate me, I was the only one in the group who wasn't incriminated. I had a different relationship to them, for both these chicks I was the man in their life. That was what saved me. The whole group, which to that point had only been half illegal, was suddenly illegalized. A few were immediately arrested. The Blues was destroyed.

With the destruction of the Blues the R.A.F. came into prominence. They had formed at about the same time we did, because they considered us totally crazy: the Blues, in other words, were complete dilettantes and fools who handled things in a totally unserious way, and were unpolitical crazies.

The state apparatus turned fully against the Blues, because from the beginning they had maintained separations even more rigidly. They vanished into apartments in new developments, with short hair, and fat cars outside the door, and they had shooting irons in their hands. They were the first ones to introduce weapons.

*Another member of the Hash Rebel scene.

We never operated with weapons, never had any, just placed bombs or threw molotovs during street fights. In that sense we had a different tactic. We came to weapons slowly, while they put them to use from the beginning.

Like the freeing of Baader, of course that had its crazy element too. The man was in the cell next to me in the joint, in the hospital at Moabit. I was there to figure out some simple escape. Connections in the joint were still lax, and you could still do a crazy lot. But he wanted no part of that number, and had had himself transferred to Tegel, where they planned the escape the other way round. Their problem was that they were always saying 'orderly actions show how things are done.'

But we always said, do an action that anyone can do. Always make the bomb so primitive that anyone else can make one too. Even if we're not around anymore, there are always people who can continue the style. Logistics have to be simplified, universal. Like the skeleton key in your pocket. You can get rocks out of cement with it, you can unlock doors with it, you can vanish with it, you can crack a cigarette machine with it, and you can steal a car. You only have a few universal things, and pass on the experience. For example, the bomb out of the drugstore. You can buy the stuff anywhere. They can't ban Vasoline, that's impossible. They can't cripple a whole branch of industry. We always did stuff like that, led a people's war with the most simple means. People's war, so that everyone can take part in it. The Viet Cong started the same way, generally all the people did, they didn't just show up with a tank somewhere. Partisan groups are built this way, slowly raising the level. Whereas they had a different rhetoric. When we said in comic strip lingo, 'A Pig's a Pig and a Pig must be offed,' to them it meant 'really going bang for a change.' In some ways, it amounts to the same thing, but at the same time we were on a more mellow level than the R.A.F. Then they pulled this giant escape, and some harmless old grandfather gets shot down. Immediately, all of them were made illegal, everyone had been legal except for Baader and Ensslin,* and so it went.

Our group was made up of proletarians. The majority were workers, except for Georg** and three or four others who were students. R.A.F., on the other hand, had only a few workers,

*Gudrun Ensslin—one of the founders of the R.A.F.
**Georg Von Rauch

and were purely a student group at the core, all intellectuals. The problem of violence was dealt with differently.

They were the first to use weapons; but they did it at an irrational time, when it was not really appropriate. An intellectual draws the moment at which he uses violence out of an abstraction: he says, I'm making revolution because of imperialism, or some other theoretical reason. And so he justifies using violence toward others—of course to some extent out of the experience of the movement he's participating in, but still primarily out of the abstract situation. That's what makes him an intellectual, he has to check things out with his head first.

We'd lived with violence from the time we were children; it has material roots. On payday, when the old man comes home drunk and beats up the old lady—it's all that stuff. At school, you get into scrapes, you have to make your way with fists, for you that's a perfectly normal thing; you fight at your workplace, you fight in bars, you have a more healthy relationship to it. For you, violence is a completely spontaneous thing that you can unroll quite easily. There was always this split between the R.A.F. and ourselves, in the source of violence, where it was coming from.

While I'm in the joint, the people outside are made so illegal that they can't continue anymore. Later, some of them are in the joint too: Georg was convicted, then Tommy (Weisbecker) sat; Zupp, Knoll, Reiche,* they all sat, were all in the joint and had trials. During the time I was in the joint, I kept trying to tell people, 'the tactic you're using is wrong. These totally senseless bombings every night aren't justifiable anymore.' I kept saying they should find another way, but in the joint you don't have much influence anymore.

In the joint itself, I acted like this: you play a little dumb, that's the best thing, then you have more freedom and can move around better. In the end, you figured that out. I read an insane amount during this time.

I gave political books to the people who were lying in the cells around me. They were all just normal criminals. I did a little joint agitation. That's the only thing you can do at all anymore, you try to organize hunger strikes. Once we even succeeded at it in Ploetzennsee, fifty people took part in it for three days, and in

*Zupp, Knoll, Reiche—members of the Hash Rebels.

the kitchen they threw over the buckets of food, and kicked up a row. Nothing happened to anyone, because we did it right. When they said, 'here are the troublemakers,' I went to them and said, 'I'm the only troublemaker, hang another one on me, I'll just laugh about it.' So they gave it up, on the spot.

The names of the prisoners who participated appeared in the *Extra-Dienst* and in *883,* and the people outside began to concern themselves with them. It was a first step for the 'Red and Black Help'* for normal prisoners. I always took part in things like that in the joint. We also said, we want more money for our work here, and other things like that.

I always saw to it that I conducted myself in such a way that I would get the chance to split, I was always playing with the idea of escaping, later, that would have been very useful too. But then they let me out. I always knew I would continue when I got out. I tried to camouflage that as far as possible. If you try miming the super-radical, they'll cut off your last possibilities of moving around in the joint. I mean, you can stand a year and a half. Actually, the suffering of the people around me disturbed me much more, because they weren't sitting in there with this kind of consciousness. It was much worse for them, and if you see the constant suicide attempts, or the successful suicides, the joint crazies tearing their cells apart, or all of those things—that always got to me more than my own situation. I could always handle it; after all, I knew why I was sitting. It was just part of the plan from the beginning: of course you knew that in some way you'd get caught. You have to be clear about that when you get involved in these things. We hadn't figured that it would go so quickly, but that it can happen somehow is clear.

I got out in the summer of '71. I got parole in the trial. During the trial it was clear that Georg was facing ten years: he had been so incriminated by Hella and Annakatrin, it was crazy. Tommy, he had gone in earlier, he wasn't incriminated as strongly, and I wasn't at all, so they let us out.

We got parole after two days of the trial. Right away, we thought of changing roles downstairs in the cell. Tommy had a long beard and curls, and Georg too, and I had medium hair

*Socialist and Anarchist relief group for the support of persecuted comrades, especially those in prison.

with a shorter beard. So when the judge says, 'here, Weisbecker and Baumann, parole,' Georg and I got up and left, and Tommy remained seated, acting as if he were Von Rauch. We created considerable chaos in the courtroom, running around hugging people and screaming—and in the chaos, Georg split.

So then downstairs in the cell, Tommy suddenly said, 'Listen, why are you taking me down here, there seems to be a total mistake, I'm Weisbecker, I was dismissed, you can't lock me up here again, you've gotta stop this.' Naturally, we had split in the meantime.

So once again there was a man out, in a perfectly simple way, through one of these sleight-of-hand tricks. Of course, it's a much better thing to get out like this, than in one of those revolver numbers. There's more wit behind it, more imagination plays a part in it.

Pig ist Pig · · · Pig muß Putt

Befreit alle Gefangenen!

Liebe Hella!
Ich möchte Dir zum erstenmal schreiben. Sei nicht böse, daß es so lange gedauert hat, aber es hat keinen Sinn, sich nur ein Hallo zuzurufen. Ich habe hier im Knast gehört, daß Du wieder verhaftet worden bist bei den Aktionen auf dem Kudamm. Du sollst mit Steinen nach Bullen geschmissen haben. Erinnerst Du Dich noch daran als wir uns das erste

Mal unterhielten − es war im Zodiak und ist jetzt bald ein Jahr her. Du sagtest damals, Du könntest uns nicht verstehen, daß wir demonstrieren, uns wehren gegen diese Pigs etc. Jetzt gehst Du auch auf die Straße und mit Dir immer mehr Typen. Du wirst sehen, daß es immer mehr Arbeiter oder wie in meinem Fall ausgeflippte Arbeiter werden, die für die eigenen Interessen kämpfen. Das Leben, wie es bisher abrollt, erscheint uns sinnlos, öde, leer und unmenschlich. Wir versuchen auf irgendeine Art auszubrechen, um Gefühle des Glücks, der Zärtlichkeit und der Gemeinsamkeit zu erleben, die uns diese bürgerliche Gesellschaft verweigert. Die Aussicht, ein ganzes Leben unter diesen herrschenden Verhältnissen leben und arbeiten zu müssen, erscheint uns derart entsetzlich, daß wir uns abwenden, zum Gift greifen und vor uns hindämmern ohne uns um irgendetwas noch zu kümmern. Aber bald müssen wir entdecken, daß uns das System auch dabei nicht in Ruhe läßt. RD-Bullen werden uns auf den Hals gejagt.
Und dann das Geldproblem. Diese vertierte Gesellschaft hat es geschafft, alles so einzurichten, daß jeder gezwungen ist, mitzumachen oder in der Gosse zu verrecken.
Ich kann hier jeden Tag die Opfer dieser Unterdrückung sehen und begreife durch deren

Keine Am-
für die
nestie
Justiz

Lebensgeschichte die Geschichte des Kapitalismus. Solange nicht die ökonomischen Verhältnisse verändert sind, solange ist ein menschliches Leben unmöglich. Es gibt nur einen Ausweg aus unserer Situation und der heißt soziale Weltrevolution, Weltbürgerkrieg. Wir müssen anstelle der Konkurrenz und des Individualismus unsere proletarische Solidarität setzen und unsere Bedürfnisse, die sich im Kampf

A PIG IS A PIG...THE PIG MUST BE OFFED!
Free All Prisoners!

Dear Hella!

I want to write to you for the first time. Don't be angry that it took so long just to say hello. I heard here in the joint that you were arrested again during the actions at the Kudamm. You're supposed to have thrown rocks at a cop. Do you remember the first time we talked—it was in the Zodiac almost a year ago now. You said then that you couldn't understand us, why we demonstrate and defend ourselves against the pigs, etc. And now you too go out on the streets and more and more guys with you. You will see that more and more workers or, as in my case, flipped out workers, will fight for their own interests. Life, as it has rolled along, seems senseless to us, vacuous, empty, and inhuman. We attempt to break out in some way in order to experience feelings of joy, of tenderness, and of community which this bourgeois society denies us. The expectation of living a whole life under existing circumstances, and to have to work, seems so horrifying that we turn away, reach for poison, and just drone along without caring about anything anymore. But we soon have to discover that the system will not leave us in peace even with this. RD pigs are put on our necks.

And then the problem of money. This bestial society has succeeded in arranging everything in such a way that everyone is forced to participate, or to die in the gutter. I can see the victims of this oppression here everyday, and through the story of their lives I understand the history of capitalism. As long as the economic conditions are not changed, a humane life is not possible. There is only one way out of our situation, and that is called social world revolution, world civil war. We have to put our proletarian solidarity in the place of competition, and satisfy our needs which will fully develop in the struggle in such a way that we become human beings who take their history in hand in order to make our own history. Instead of alienated capitalist labor, which is only for profit, we must and we will build a means of work based on the satisfaction of peoples' needs. In short, it's a matter of creating the man of the 21st century, like Che says in his legacy to us. We will fulfill this legacy, cost what it will! Like Eldridge Cleaver says: "We will be human beings. We will be, or the world will be flattened in our attempt to become so." See you soon!   Bommi

WORDS CANNOT SAVE US!

WORDS DON'T BREAK CHAINS!

THE DEED ALONE MAKES US FREE!

DESTROY WHAT DESTROYS YOU!

HELLA   ANNEKATRIN

Der Abend

26. Jahr · Nr. 156   FREITAG   9. Juli 1971

Mit Brillen-Trick in die Freiheit

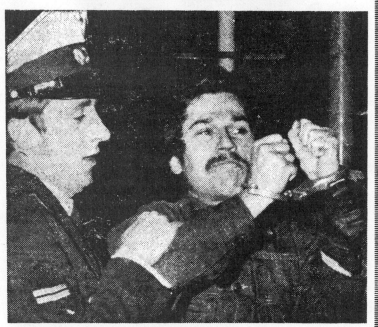

IN HANDCUFFS: The 22-year old Thomas Weisbecker

INTO FREEDOM
WITH A SPECTACLES TRICK

* The 24-year old Georg Von Rauch, who succeeded in fleeing from the Moabit Criminal Court yesterday noon through a clever trick, seems to be swallowed up by the Earth. A massive search started immediately by the Security and Criminal Police remained without results. Only the co-defèndant, 22-year old Thomas Weisbecker, could be taken into custody in his apartment in Schoeneberg. He is accused of aiding in the escape of the prisoner.

The flight of Georg Von Rauch, who together with Weisbecker and the 23-year old Michael "Bommi" Baumann was in court as a result of the attack on the "Quick" reporter Horst Rieck in February 1970, is not without comedy. Since the proceedings were postponed to the 16th of July in order to provide further evidence, the Court agreed to the release on bail of Baumann and Weisbecker. Only Von Rauch was to go back to the U-Prison because he also faced charges in the Chamber Court for arson, and because he had 48 days on a parole violation from an opium offense.

Two defendants left the defense table immediately after the announcement of dismissal, mixed with the audience, and left the hall. As the marshall then attempted to lead away the presumed Georg Von Rauch, he declared: "I'm Thomas Weisbecker."

Indeed, Weisbecker and Von Rauch have a strong resemblance. And in order to make an even bigger fool of the marshall, Weisbecker had Von Rauch give him his glasses at the end of the proceedings and put them on.

When the representatives of justice finally noticed that they had let the wrong one go free, it was already too late to set off the alarm. No one cared about Thomas Weisbecker anymore, even though there was a strong suspicion that he had at least aided in the escape. He too could leave the court unhindered. Only sometime later did the police carry on a search for him. There was a warrant for his arrest only after the marshall testified that his answer to their express question was very clearly that he was Georg Von Rauch.

The fugitive Georg Von Rauch is approximately 1.78 meters, has shoulder long, dark, unkempt hair, and a full beard. When he vanished from Criminal Court he wore a red shirt without collar with a black yoke, dark blue corduroy jeans with a dark belt, and a black scarf. He presumably has changed his appearance in the meantime. The police warned that the 24-year old may be armed, which according to them is not unlikely.

As it was reported, Georg Von Rauch is accused in the trial now going on of having forced his way, together with Bommi Baumann, Thomas Weisbecker, and others, into the apartment of the Illustrated's reporter Horst Rieck on Fasanen Street in Charlottenburg, and having abused the 29-year old. During the main proceeding, Von Rauch had not responded at all until now to this accusation.

HES

Georg v. Rauch

CHAPTER EIGHT

The June 2nd Movement

Then we were outside, and a few who had been waiting outside joined us, and some who had come to the point where they said, 'We want to do stuff like this,' and overnight, we were a troop of ten people again.

We began to reconstruct. But because the situation had accelerated so far, we had to get on the trip of doing something like what the R.A.F. was doing. We had to get guns, illegal houses and cars, and then as our next action, we thought of freeing a prisoner, because at the moment we were so weak.

I saw that it was going to go a hundred percent wrong—this is the big fat end. I only participated out of solidarity, and I said, because I agitated for such a long time and held the reins, we'll deal with the consequences together. Now it didn't matter anymore if we dug out teeth into a sour apple. The action was unnecessary, that was clear to me.

Before I went into the joint, the general mood was completely different: people were still behind us. But in the meantime, a climate had been created in which the R.A.F. and its methods were denounced by many leftists. Hardly anyone supported us by the time we got out.

So we said, we'll do it differently than R.A.F.—we'll stay in one city, we'll stay in Berlin, because we know our way around here best. And we won't run around somewhere in West Germany in B.M.W.'s.

We took Kreuzberg* as our base. The social structure there had changed so that there were almost only Turks** there, lumpen-proletarians and a few really poor working class families with a lot of children (insofar as that still exists in Germany†),

---

*Kreuzberg is a very old and poor neighbourhood in Berlin.
**Turks constitute a sizeable portion of the migrant labor force.
†Most of the lowest-paid menial work is done by migrant workers and not by Germans.

and dropouts. That's the only poverty district in Berlin. Kreuzberg is the worst district somehow.

Our former base, including the whole Hash Rebel scene, had become dope and Hari Krishna* and the like, and there wasn't really anything left to do with them anymore. To the outside, they appeared at best as macro-apostles, or came on us as Hari Krishna monks. You really can't say to these people, hey we're making a revolution—they'll only say, 'old buddy, Hari Krishna.'

We started to get involved with the apprentices and young workers in the Kreuzberg. On the one hand we tried to make contacts with them, and on the other, with factory groups such as the Proletarian Left, who were building up cadres in factories, as well as with the Kreuzberg district group, who were occupying a youth center. Those were our contacts toward the outside.

We began to build up our infrastructure again. We were all legal in the beginning, except for Georg. So we could still drive around, we still had the name; we tried to anchor ourselves in these community groups, and from there push forward the strategy of armed struggle. We performed perfectly normal agitation work there—for example, going from door to door and gathering signatures against the senseless reclamation politics of the senate. As well, we were meeting in preparation for militant night and fog actions.

Later, we gave ourselves the name June 2nd, chosen first of all to differentiate ourselves from R.A.F. And June 2nd was the day Ohnesorg was shot to death by the pig Kurras. In the news announcements it was always mentioned that June 2nd was the day he got it. So one could clearly show' 'you fired the first shot; if there's any shooting back, it's what you deserve.' So it couldn't always be said that the people bring violence. Violence rules, from birth to the grave, and it is simply heightened if you fight against it—it becomes totally concrete. This is what the name was to symbolize.

The June 2nd group had a theoretical base similar to 'Gauche Proletarienne'** in France, or 'Lotta Continua'† in Italy—that

---

*One of the largest esoteric Eastern religious cults which became popular in the West in the late '60's.
**Extreme left French organization with whom Sartre sympathized. Has not existed since 1972.
†Extreme left Italian organization that grew out of the workers' struggles of 1969. Now tends towards sectarian Marxist-Leninist party-building.

is, to give a militant solution to work conflicts in the factories. When the people in factories are falling over from the bad air, then the owner's villa must be put on fire, to show the people you can defend yourself if you attack the guy directly; the character mask is human, and therefore damageable, and if you hit him in his private life, that's precisely where he'll be scared back. But it never got to that point. Or you bomb the offices of a man like Mosch who makes outrageous speculations and land reclamations, so-called, at the expense of the people.*

We took part in the mass actions against the B.V.G. [Berlin Public Transit system] price raise. B.V.G. ticket machines were destroyed. This was the sort of basic guerrilla work which we influenced. Painting up B.V.G. buses, leaflets, stick-ons. We had nothing to do with the bomb in the B.V.G. building, one of the few bombs we didn't approve.

To develop militance in the community groups, and in the factories, to develop factory guerrillas from that source, is to become urban guerrillas in the truest sense of the word.

Then to deal with the problem of guest workers. We had contact with left groups of guest workers too. To always put forward their demands militantly, to focus on the possibility of armed revolution from there and push it forward. Guest workers: imperialism as it takes place among us. Hitler said that one day the hordes of Asiatic sub-humans would be herded into our factories and work here. Then they will be amazed at the monumental greatness of German power. And that's what's happening now, when some Turk stands in front of the Siemens building and looks up—Hitler's words have been horrifyingly fulfilled. Let's not fool ourselves about what's happening here.

Leaflets, demos, stick-ons, neighborhood aid, a sort of red assistance in the communities on the one hand, and also getting involved with the problems of youth centers.

And on the other hand, supporting a clandestine cell, which is not recognized, whose cadre do the night and fog actions and support mass actions through them.

This then was the political work we envisioned and took in hand. It wasn't a matter of abstractly building a Red Army. If it

*Land speculations were at a peak at this time in Germany.

isn't rooted from the beginning, I just don't know what it's supposed to do. It can only react abstractly. But only a few people were still in support of this terrorist stuff, and trying to connect it with other similar groups in order to once again establish a common strategy which would be successful. But building up such an apparatus just didn't work. A guerrilla apparatus that is already at a higher stage of development makes so many demands on you that you don't have time for other things. The logistics work makes incredibly many demands, and we had just come out with only the clothes on our backs, not a single Mark, nothing.

At first, a few people still gave us money, or offered us a place to live.

Later we started cracking open cigarette machines, out of need or other similar nonsense because we just had nothing left to eat. We went out, we didn't have a single Mark, stood in front of the light shows in Kreuzberg on Wiener Street and cracked open a cigarette machine. Of course there wasn't a Mark in it. But immediately all these people come out and clean out the cigarette machine, and we were the nice sugar-daddies with the cigarettes.

We still thought we'd get our feet on the ground in Berlin, and could manage longer here.

Then we got to the point of doing bank robberies and simply getting our money that way. That is already a different form of action, because for the first time you appear with a weapon.

Until this point you've just done night and fog actions. You learn to conduct yourself quietly on the street, to check out a target, to observe, to sneak up on it, or to steal a car and siphon gasoline. You learn to move in this manner.

With a bank, of course, it's a totally different story, because you appear openly in the daytime. You're totally visible, and that is a new thing, a new experience.

So we started checking out this bank and checking out the escape routes. The bank was still possible, it's still possible as long as this glass box which they put around everything still has an opening that you can stick the weapon into. This place had it.

So we went in early in the morning and there happened to be snow flurries, totally favorable weather. Of course, we had dressed up so noticeably that we almost died laughing when we saw ourselves in the glass in front of the bank. Our own masquerade was just so impossible again! Then we stormed in with a loud hello, and chased the man out of the cash box, screaming. We just didn't have any idea about things like that, we made totally crazy demands, hands up or not.

I stood at the door and this old grandma comes in and I say to her, 'Come on in, come on in, there's a raid going on right now.' And she just looks at me, a dear little old woman, and grins at me, and looks at my pistol. I automatically grinned back, I thought she was pretty good. I had one of these scarves tied over my face, we really looked impossible. But the old woman was far out, there was this really spontaneous communication with her.

When you're standing there like that, you develop a whole new set of instincts; first of all, you feel insanely secure, it's logical because you have this weapon. Of course, it's horrible, a little pistol like that, a weapon, it has its own dynamics. You just feel insanely secure because you have a thing like that in your hand. As well, you feel secure because the element of surprise is on your side, as far as you can see it you're in control. It all goes insanely fast.

But then the alarm was set off in this thing, they have these little switches everywhere, and we say, okay, we're splitting. But somehow it's quite weird, people begin to talk to you, someone said, 'It was your fault that the alarm was set off.' There is a very peculiar atmosphere in a bank like that. You start developing an instinct for such things. You know exactly what's going on. It's not like a night and fog action, where you look around and do something; in a thing like this you act differently, you act completely instinctively. Of course, your years of experience help you—since you've been doing things like that, you can change in a split second, you know exactly how you need to act.

The Samurai story is the best example of this, from the film *The Seven Samurai,* where the one fighter recruits the others by hiding a fighter behind the door and saying to the applicants, 'Why don't you come in?' With the first one, he snaps the whip right in front of his head, and of course he fails the test. The second one can barely ward off the whip, and the third one says,' 'Come out from behind the door, you can't fool me.'

It is precisely this instinct for doing the right thing unconsciously that's actually the highest form you can reach in this guerrilla business, developing instincts like an animal in the jungle. This comes out for the first time in business like the bank. You sort of stand beside yourself and watch what you're doing, it's like an acid experience again.

If you feel secure, things will go well, too. If you look for your security in technology, it can always fail you. Of course, it's logical, you have a lot less influence on it than you do on yourself. You have to plan the escape, you have to know how you're going to get yourself out.

That's what we did, too, and got through safely. A couple of times we drove past police barricades. Then you see how they jump out of the car, totally scared, stand on the curb, close the intersection with their submachineguns, and you drive past them laughing in a B.V.G. bus. There's no danger for you anymore.

When I got back to the illegal apartment, I had all the change from the bank. There was a beggar by the apartment door. He was standing there with his hat in his hand, and asked if I had any money, and I say, 'Sure, old man, you'll never believe what kind of money I have,' and then filled his hat with all the change. It fell on the street, just rolled out of the hat, since I had all my pockets full. Of course, the guy totally flipped out over me, he said, I hope you live a long time, and that I was the nicest person in the world, and I said to him, 'Old man, it's incredible fun. It's very simple in life, you just have to be in the right place at the right time. It happened to me that way, and now it's happening to you too. Take it easy.' And then I went on.

Then in the apartment, you listen to the police radio, and hear exactly what amounts you took; you don't even have to bother counting it.

The experiences in a bank robbery are precisely these instinctive things, that you can experience fully only in praxis. Later, in all these massive searches, it helped me incredibly that you're automatically instinctively secure when you move outside, even in the greatest confusion. Even in an apartment like that, you know for sure you're not being watched; you don't depend on technology all the time, locked into a thousand codes, camouflaged, on a thousand things, like the Baader-Meinhof—

that's exactly what you don't do. You've learned to live on the street, because you've always been illegal in some way with these petty criminal things—you're the Blues. That's precisely the thing you've learned, that you don't need all this apparatus, you don't get involved with all that shit.

That was the mistake of R.A.F., that they opposed the apparatus of the bulls with their own apparatus, which is always weaker. The opposition just has much longer experience in this area, and they also have bigger, better apparatus—that's precisely their thing, because that's what they invented, the methods of gathering material, identification, etc. And they've got a computer to do it, so they're really better, that's where they're at, that's where they're the big specialists.

Not a single one of them is Blues; they can't deal with the way you act, doing exactly what no one expects, all of the time. For example, running around in all those bright clothes so that everyone thinks: one of those insane Hash brothers, some crazy. It happened to me a couple of times; I'd get caught in a street barricade, and always get through, even with stolen cars or a motorcycle, because they said, a bird like that would never have anything to do with this. So I always got through. Once, the car was brightly painted, and on the back, in big letters was written: 'Careful, Dynamite Transporter!' And there really were bombs in it, and they just looked at it and said, 'Dynamite Transporter!—Idiot. Just go on.' And it really was one! You carried things to such an extreme, it was so open that no one bought it anymore. If that's the trip you're on, no one can deal with that kind of craziness.

Of course, you learn the technology of these things: falsifying all sorts of passes and stamps, making exact prints, you become a total forger. You become a specialist in cracking car locks, you can crack a car in half a minute these days. You become a very good weapons specialist, you know how to handle weapons wonderfully, take them apart, clean them, better than any soldier. And you become a very good planner, every criminal in the movies dreams of this. You see whether a bank is breakable or not when you walk past it. That means no specialization. Everyone must be able to do everything.

If someone survives, and recruits new people, he can

immediately pass on the wealth of experience that a guerrilla group like this has. You're already a new quality, you're no longer a specialist like you were earlier. People had a passport forger, a bomb specialist, and a weapons specialist then. You're a specialist in every field. You're a planner as well as an executor; you can do it as well as put it together, and you know how to conduct it; you kow how to handle radio, you can change radios into police transmitters. You learn everything, you must know everything.

A further reason is that no authoritarian structures can be created. If everyone has the same expectations, it's impossible to say, I'm the boss here, that authority no longer exists. A lot of authority is hacked away.

The person who has the most power and the least abrasion as a result of pressures from outside, he'll still have the final word; so in a situation like that, you never totally eliminate the hierarchy of authority.

When new people wanted to participate, there was always the difficulty that you had had longer experience, and the thing was clear to you. I had already faced death, and I had already been in the joint. Then dimensions of the joint and of death naturally played a completely subordinate role for me, because I had had concrete experience with it, which I could re-evaluate for myself. To the new people you said, 'Listen old man, in the best case, a couple of years in the joint at the end, in the other case, an incredibly quiet place in the cemetery, so you've won.' It was never really figured out that you couldn't really transmit something like that through words, because it's a concrete experiential value which cannot be made in any other way.

You aren't able to let people die beforehand. The shamans and the old priests of Egypt did that. They let their people die symbolically, through drugs, and then were totally secure that the guy would follow their path. But we never had control of such treasures of technology.

We saw the will to participate, and tried to estimate psychic structures as far as you can do that, from your vantage point. And mistakes kept appearing, because you never saw how heavy the thing would become, where the flops would be. You're carrying the devil's cloven hoof with you.

'Don't freak out, the bank's this way!' 'Wait! I wanna clean out this candy store first!' 'Hey! What am I s'posed to do? I've never even *been* in a bank.'

Taken from Those Fabulous Furry Freak Brothers Comix.

CHAPTER NINE

The Death of Georg

I want to discuss the interview with *Spiegel* once again, because a great many people thought badly of me—that is, the left did. They took what I said badly.

I have to say today that I no longer know who first pulled the trigger. I believed it was Georg, but after all the confusion, I really can't remember anymore. In any case, one thing I find really shitty is that the left simply begins with the assumption that Georg didn't pull the trigger at all. The left has made a real Christian martyr—a real Christian humanity trip is what's coming off. The guy wasn't like that, he was the kind of guy who said, 'of course we'll shoot.' We had the gun with us so that we wouldn't be arrested anymore. That's why we had the things with us, and not so that we could stand there with our hands up and be shot down in a row. That's precisely what we didn't want. The bulls were shooting at everybody. As a result of the Baader-Meinhof stuff, the climate among the bulls had gotten to such a place that they always 'knew' that we were armed and that there would be shooting.

Already once before Urbach had given us weapons; thus the Security Police delivered weapons with which the police would be shot down. That's the situation in Germany. It's very perverted. We basically didn't see that we were marionettes on strings. When they themselves put the weapons in our hands, then they're very interested that they be used, too. No one thought about that, nobody except the groups who criticized us for giving fuel to fascism, in order to rationalize their own trip.

In 1968, Nollau [of the Federal News Service] said that the task of the Security Police is to support all Maoist groups. They put weapons into our hands, so that we can off their own people. It isn't clear to me even today what role one plays in that game. But it looks different from an independent revolutionary movement. Somehow the pigs are very interested in our doing it.

That should be followed further, that fine thread. I mean, I don't have a concrete answer to that, but all of us should think about it.

The concrete happening itself, that was our mistake. There was a massive search just the day before, because of the eternal banks. Our stolen cars were flying around everywhere, and twenty packages of guns and bombs from Baader-Meinhof had just appeared in one apartment. Right at that moment, they called a massive search. They hermetically sealed Berlin—all the access roads, the airports, the train stations—and flew in a whole security force. All the streets were closed. We found out about it at night, and went to bed, got up in the morning, smoked a couple of joints, and Georg suddenly says, 'Ouch, we still have a car standing there, a Ford bus—we have to move it so they don't get it.' They're very hard to rip off, a different kind of lock. They're harder to steal than other cars, and we needed that one over and over again. It was our most important car, we transported everything in it. We just hadn't realized that it was insanity to let that car disappear in that situation. We immediately leave the house, get into a car, drive over, and climb into this shit Ford bus.

This was a double*—you constantly played their game with insanity like that too. As an illegal group in Berlin, it's crazy to use cars at all. Only in actions with some sort of getaway, otherwise never—subway, bus, walking, taxi—never use a car. We never quite grasped that.

But even if you're making doubles, that's exactly the area in which cops are always better, because they have the greatest technical means. They can always find you as a result of those numbers. They simply say, there's a stolen car, then they drive around, because they know that the license plates are gonna be duplicated, and they simply note all the double numbers.

The original bus had a label on it, the one we had didn't. It was standing at the Winterfeldplatz, and of course was immediately conspicuous. The guy who had already discovered thousands of stolen cars in Berlin discovered it; he always takes part in B.Z. searches*. He saw that the number was a double. A

*A stolen car with a license plate from a legal car of the same type.
**Daily column in the Berlin paper *Bild-Zeitung,* listing the numbers of stolen cars.

policeman was standing at every car that was in question during these hours. The great search ran for 24 hours—our photos were everywhere, on television, on every newsflash, on the evening news; it went on constantly. The whole city was made hysterical, first one day of quiet search, and then a massive open search.

So then we got in the car, and as we're parking it on Eisenacher Street, a plainsclothes cop puts his gun up under our noses. We're made to stand up against the wall. As the pig gets distracted for a moment, this insane shooting starts.

We ran, and they chased us through Berlin for three hours with dogs, and cars, and honk, honk, honk. On foot we ran down the whole Kudamm, with bulls constantly around us, but Hari Krishna will save us! We run toward the Kranzlereck, and there we see that they've already started to close it off, just shut down the whole Kudamm at that moment, put a whole bunch of VW busses across it, and jump out with their machine guns. We're just getting there, and while we're thinking about where to run now, a whole troop of Hari Krishna monks stops us and says, here, Hari Krishna, and try to sell us their brochures, and I say, 'Old man, let me go, I'm gonna knock you over, are you crazy?' they were after us too. They hold us up for about one minute in front of the Wertheim department store, shortly before the Kranzlereck, and during that time they arrest two others at the Kranzlereck and open up the intersection again, and we keep running. Then we hid in a couple of apartments, and then split.

The flight was touchy, because the pigs put through the radio not that Georg was shot, but one of their men. Then it immediately came through, don't make any more arrests: that means if they get you, they'll just shoot you down. We heard that over the police radio, in those apartments.

The problem looks like this, that you're now standing in these apartments, and the people who live there are with you. So you pull these people along into an absolute stream of violence. At that moment, they'll be done in with you one hundred percent. You're not only putting yourself in danger, there'll be indiscriminate smashing. Of course, you can take this into consideration and say, even more people will be put off. And indignation is precisely one of the most important revolutionary moments: it explains to the people that they can be indignant (Bakunin), but even when you shoot your way free, if you leave the dead behind, that's even worse.

This is only to say, we don't need to create a Christian martyr here. We have said, we'll take weapons in hand, and run up against the system, and of course we'll shoot first. That's why we carry the things along. When we're in that situation, we shoot, logically. The brother fell in the struggle, for that thing for which the people with the red flags go into the street—for that, he fell in the struggle with his weapon in his hand. They should see him as such, and not as a Christian martyr again. They should see him for what he was, an Anarchist who fell in the struggle, who followed through straight to the end. Of course, that didn't come out in the shit *Spiegel* interview, because they shortened it so much. I don't care about anything except saying that.

Of course, after that I was completely done in, because I had started all these things together with him, I always had the strongest relationship with him, and was with him all those years. I literally saw him fall over next to me, and you knew right on the spot that he was dead. When he fell over, I knew: now he's gone. It was a week before I could eat or sleep—a week before I could see through it clearly, I was really flipping out. Periodically I was really out of it, and just couldn't figure anything out anymore.

Then I saw in the conduct of the other people that there wasn't any warmth anymore. No one really understood me in my situation, and no one wanted to get into it. I had to let myself be told: now your best friend is gone, it's your own fault. You just don't know what you can do anymore. You see then that the death of your brother has been taken the same way as the Springer press presented it. No one approaches it in the human way appropriate in a situation like that. At most they say, 'these pigs, we have to get our revenge,' nothing more. Because he was built up as a martyr, not even this moment of revenge came out right, only this pity.

That was the first time I thought about the whole thing taking on forms that have nothing to do with its origins: neither with the commune business, nor with our dropouts in the '60's, nor with our Blues and Hash Rebels, nor with our drug experiences, nor with our sexual experiences, nothing about our new sensibility and tenderness and understanding, getting into another person, it has nothing do with all that anymore. It just got crazier, it got more and more like a hall in a Siemens* factory, all the things that happened.

Even though the whole thing was about getting yourself away from Siemens, suddenly you're right there again. You're standing there with short hair, with a suit, with everything the same again as where you came from; and the people around you react in the same way, they're just as hardened as you. So you wore yourself out all those years, and did everything, and suddenly you arrive right back there again.

So I started to see less and less sense in it. I actually participated because of Georg, because I just knew he wanted to do these things, and I didn't want to leave him alone.

Three days later, some people in Kreuzberg occupied a house and called it Georg von Rauch House. Those were the only people who dealt with it adequately.

*Siemens, like Ford in the U.S., represents the ultimate in alienated assembly line work.

„Freunde, schmeißt die Knarre weg"

"FRIENDS, THROW AWAY THE GUN"

SPIEGEL—Interview with the Underground Anarchist Michael Baumann

SPIEGEL: Do you have a pistol in your pocket?

BAUMANN: I haven't carried a weapon with me for a year and a half now. I feel better, more free, since then. A weapon can become your worst enemy.

SPIEGEL: In a poem which you composed, you said it like this, "I've put away the gun, friends, because I've come to the recognition that hatred is not your driving force, but that love is—love is my driving force." It almost sounds a little corny for an Anarchist.

* * *

SPIEGEL: Were you afraid?

BAUMANN: Fear? More likely the desire for adventure. I sensed a thrill which dangerous experiences can have. One never totally experiences fear.

SPIEGEL: Was it People's War for you?

BAUMANN: We never quite saw it that seriously. Actually it was fun. We laughed a lot about our costuming. I looked like a comic clown.

SPIEGEL: There are two dead on the path you walked: the boat-builder Beelitz, who lost his life as a result of one of the bombs which you helped to build, and Georg von Rauch, who was shot by the police in West Berlin on Eisenacher Street in your presence.

BAUMANN: Those are ending points. Those are dead men who bring one to a recognition. In Beelitz's case, there was horror; with Georg von Rauch, there was hatred once again. Once you see him falling, next to you, then you see him falling for a pretty long time.

SPIEGEL: Does one see him falling before that too?

BAUMANN: One saw the possibility, yes, yes.

SPIEGEL: Who shot first on Eisenacher Street?

BAUMANN: Of course, Georg, but there was shooting almost simultaneously.

SPIEGEL: When did you shoot?

BAUMANN: When you hear a shot, you shoot back automatically, that's logical.

SPIEGEL: And now? "Bommi" the bomber is passe?

BAUMANN: I'm back where I started off now, and I still feel like a part of a movement that seeks its fortune outside of this society by other roads, in a great stream. Look, the prodigal son returns? That's not going to happen.

SPIEGEL: You're not going to turn yourself into the police?

BAUMANN: No, not under any circumstances. And why? I've already sat in prison for eighteen months. I don't need to have that experience again, and they're not gonna solve my problems there either. If you look at all of this for awhile, from a distance, in peace, then you start getting a different picture of the world. If you're not the blind man anymore, then the boatman waits for you who will bring you to the other shore.

SPIEGEL: The Garden of Eden underground? Where does it go?

BAUMANN: There are concrete alternatives. I can't name my alternatives to you, because then they wouldn't be there anymore.

Der Anruf bei 110: „Es wird geschossen, schnell Mensch!"

Tonband-Protokoll des ersten Alarms bei der Funkbetriebszentrale der Polizei zur Schießerei Eisenacher Straße

---

The Call on 110: THERE'S SHOOTING, HURRY UP, MAN!

Radio Log of the first alarm at the Central radio Control of the Police for the shoot-out on Eisenacher Street.

The police have only reported their own versions of the shoot-out on the 4th of December on Eisenacher Street in Schoeneberg during which Georg Von Rauch was killed, and the results of the interrogation of the slightly injured policeman. We have now listened to Central Radio Control's log of the first witness who called on the emergency 110. This witness, along with his wife, looked down on to Eisenacher Street from the third story balcony of his house and noticed the proceedings even before the first shots were fired. While his wife was watching the proceedings from the balcony, the witness called the Central Radio Control and passed on what his wife was describing to him. The balcony is about 200 meters from the site of the conversation that began at 17:24 hours. The receiving policeman in Central Radio Control will be designated P; the witness Z.

Z: On Eisenacher, at the corner of Fugger, three young people are being threatened with a pistol. I don't know if that's already the result of the Baader chase. Could you drive over there immediately? (The witness is speaking sensibly, even if with a little excitement in his voice. It sounds as if he just considers it too improbable that something is taking place before his eyes which heretofore he has only seen in Wild West films.

P: "Eisenacher corner..." The officer asks back with detachment and distance.

Z: Fugger, the antique store across the street from the playground.

P: What's there?

Z: (Seemingly irritated) Well, three young people are being threatened by someone with a pistol. They're leaning against the wall, um...with raised arms and like... (the voice of the caller is still quiet however, full of amazement at what is happening)

P: Threatened with a pistol, yes?

Z: (He is further informed by his wife—the voice of his wife can also be heard on the tape, however, it is difficult to understand.) By a civilian, not a policeman.

P: We're coming over.

Z: (Suddenly screams shrilly into the telephone) There's shooting, hurry up, man!

The shots could not be heard on the tape.

P: Yes, please stay on the line.

Z: (Beside himself) One of them's lying down, one of them's lying down, there's shooting, can you hear, can you hear, can you hear? One of them's shot!

P: What's your number?

Z: (Confusedly says his number, makes a mistake, and repeats his number)

P: Stay calm, the radio car is already on its way.

Z: We're looking down from the balcony, hurry up now...oh man. My nerves are shot.

P: Stay real calm, the radio car is on its way, can you give a description of the culprits?

Z: No, I can't, nothing, absolutely nothing, we live too far away from it, we're on the third story here.

P: Where are they now?

Z: (Who misunderstands the officer) I'm at home.

P: Yes, I mean the culprits.

Z: (Asks his wife) Where are the culprits now? (Repeats the questions to his wife who can clearly be heard over the phone) One of them ran away. At the corner.

P: Where to?

Z: The direction of Fugger Street. Running in the direction of Fugger Street. One in the direction of Fugger, one in the direction of Kliest.

P: Please stay on, I just have to announce something.

17:26 o'clock

Z: Someone is cleaning his car downstairs. One of them is lying there, he's lying there. (To his wife) Come here a minute, go to the telephone...when they come. They're already on their way.

The wife speaks into the telephone. The officer however is not back on the phone. "Hello. Yes that couldn't have been the police. Oh God, man."

P: Are you still on?

Again the witness.

Z: One of them is probably dead. He is lying there motionless.

P: Someone is lying there?

Z: Dead, in front of the store, across from the playground.

P: Stay on the phone.

Z: Yes, okay, yes.

P: The fire company is already on the way.

Z: It's a crazy thing, and these people are continuing to clean their car as if nothing had happened, and these people are perfectly calm as though nothing had happened. I don't understand.

P: What a shame.

Z: Right next to it, someone is cleaning his car.

P: That's the times today.

Central Radio Control spoke with the witness for four minutes, from 17:24 o'clock until 17:28. The shots sounded at 17:25. From 17:26 on, approximately 15 more calls about the shooting came to Central Radio Control. Most callers were questioned by the officers immediately after the verification, after it was explained to them that the radio car was already underway to the scene of the incident.

At 17:28 o'clock, the first radio car arrived at Eisenacher Street, then five other cars, until 17:38 o'clock. It was not easy to send a large number of radio cars to the scene on this Saturday night, open for shopping. In addition, another ten radio cars were sent in the assumed direction of the suspects' flight.

CHAPTER TEN

The Last Phase

Shortly after Georg's death, our group split up. The one group continued and kept breaking into banks, and we went totally back to the base, and broke off the guerrilla trip as such.

Those eternal bank jobs, they became a totally independent bag, with no relationship to the base anymore. Instead of the earlier abstract throwing of bombs into U.S. firms, police cars, leasing companies—everything was bombed and put on fire— then, banks were held up uninterruptedly; then that was the praxis.

The split among us began over money. Of course, you suddenly have an insane mountain of money that you just can't use anymore. The magic of money plays a role which one way or the other has a very practical effect in this society, as you can see. Of course, it plays the same role in a group like this.

When there's money around, everyone says, let's get this or that. So unnecessary things are bought, consumer articles too. So you say, if I'm gonna sit here all day anyway, then let's get a record player, and then twenty L.P.'s, and play them. And after a while, there's a television in the corner, and on a whole different level, you're a part of that whole department store trip. Or you say, we have to listen to the police radio anyway, then why not get Toshiba radios, real big, and get three of them. So you have one in every apartment. You get a whole mountain of radios, you can almost open a whole store with them, a whole bunch of nonsense like that. Or we got an entire parking lot full of cars, so that people wondered about our parking a new car outside every day; thank God no one in the house betrayed us. We lived there for over a year, they were always quiet, they all found us good, they all knew who we were, but anywhere else, it would have been noticeable. Baader-Meinhoff was hit many times as a result of that, when someone at some point noticed what was going on.

The more you make yourself illegal, that is to say, the further you isolate yourself, the more secret the things you are doing become, the more you fall right into this consumerism. Of course, you can't run around like you did before, so you keep getting more velvet suits, and at the end you look like you've jumped right out of *Playboy*.

At that point, our faction said, we'd rather give the money to the people at the base.

You can't expect some little apprentice to hold up a bank. Not everyone in Berlin can become a bank robber. Throwing a molotov against the water hose at a demo, okay, but that every 17-year old apprentice should go running into a bank, that's crazy.

So we started to divide up the money. We bought printing equipment for comrades, and we let some money flow into left organizations. There were endless hassles as a result of that, and at some point we just said, okay, you're there, we're here, and went totally back into the base.

At that time, we got it together once again to have our troop in the Kreuzberg. Sometimes we slept in the Rauch House, because the people didn't know who we were.

They thought we all slept there, but we just happened to be at the movies at the other end of town that night, and crashed somewhere else. So they moved in on them with 800 men, turned the whole house upside down, and closed off the whole Kreuzberg. We were at the other end of town, and first read about it in the paper the next day. So we escaped arrest again, by one of those flukes. Of course, an informant who had recognized us and tipped off the bulls was involved in this. In a group that large, you can't quite check that out anymore.

Of course, it was crazy of us, but we tried once more to get as close as possible to the base. Doing irrational things like that already shows how muddled you are.

The fact that I could move pretty freely in a scene like that kept me at it for another half to three-quarters of a year. A couple of actions took place, but after that it pretty much crumbled.

The final break was after the massive raid on the Rauch House—that was the absolute division into factions. Then we stopped. Since then, we haven't done much, at most, some stuff with passports, or helping some group of foreigners, but nothing else.

And then they shot Tommy, too—who'd been tried with Georg and me—so I was the last survivor from that trial. Naturally, I did another action—that's clear.

The general animosity toward pleasure slowly allowed the thing to break. More and more guys dropped out as a result.

Then we took R.A.F.'s accusations into account. They said, you're running through endless numbers of apartments, you keep fucking women and smoking hashish—no doubt that's fun for you, but this thing *can't* be fun for you, this here is a difficult job.

For me, what lies behind that attitude is the rigidity of being a student: it's this total opposition to pleasure. Every ecstasy—without which a revolution just can't happen—is lacking. In the Paris Commune, they climbed on the barricades singing, and not with a sour face, or membership cards in their pockets. They didn't say, we must make a revolution here; they said, this is our hour now, either yes or no. That's where the ecstasy lay—that on one hand, it doesn't matter to you, but that nonetheless somewhere you're still alive.

They couldn't see that it was exactly this—the mini-insanity, the gags, that brought comedy into the situation—that made the thing at least in part still worth living for and carried on the Blues feeling of life. It's these so-called flops, it's those, that's how you learn best.

So we ripped off a car, and found an 'object' in it who turned out to be a pile of laughs, but only when pressed. It was one of those totally quiet, new apartment developments. This bum started laughing repulsively, a whole uproar started while we were trying to be so quiet, so then we stepped on him and he laughed real viciously in the ditch by the street. "Ho, ho, ho." So we had to clear the field, and immediately the lights went on.

Or these frustrations: you met some chick, were terribly taken with her, and made out with her in some hallway somewhere. You could never go anywhere with her and fuck. Either it was winter, or you couldn't go to your illegal apartment. But these things were all fun. You re-experienced the sexuality of your youth again.

But you were mad if your disguise was pretty credible in itself, but at the same time so shitty that no woman would look at you. So you thought, I have a perfect disguise, but I look like a turkey in it. So you were mad again, and said, man, some other disguise. And then you run off right away to invent some other mask.

You had these breaks all the time, of course. They kept the thing alive. It was precisely these weird little flips that made it possible for you, so that at the end, you regretted nothing.

Contact With the Population

We lived in a house where everyone knew who we were, because the pictures were in the paper. Everyone knew what we were doing. No one ever ran to the police. They were mostly Turks, very few Germans.

There were people too—for example, a taxi driver who told a guy after a bank number, 'You're just coming from a bank, come on, be honest! I'll drive you anyway. I think what you're doing is really right on.' Of course, you meet people like that, who say, 'sure I'll drive you away, the bulls just give me trouble.'

For two days there was a guy painting the windows in our house. The first day we just simply talked to him. The huge Baader-Meinhof search after the bombing attacks was going on. The next morning, he knocks on the door again, and turns the radio on. They're just broadcasting live the arrest of Andy Baader and Holger Meins and Jan-Carl Raspe* in the garage in Frankfurt. He finishes painting the windows and I say to him, 'I'll come on down with you.' While we're standing on the street, he says, 'Listen, I wish you a lot of luck now so they don't catch you too; don't think I don't know what you're doing up there.'

You really did meet people like that. When someone is in your apartment for two days, in a strange apartment like that, he just catches on. When he puts the radio on the table early in the morning, and you hear them shooting, you hear someone scream when he's being shot, he can see it in your face how you're reacting to it. No other person reacts like you do; you react differently because emotionally your relationship to it is so strong. The guy notices that and says, okay.

Or you sometimes heard conversations on the street—people saying, 'What they're doing is all right.'

*June 1, 1972.

Informants

Informants like Hella or Annekatrine, right up to Brockmann at the end, who was with us for years, but despite that dropped out; it kept happening over and over again.

We were never successful at keeping sensibility in the group—the pressure from the outside was so great it caught up with you. That's where the failure of the urban guerrillas in the metropolis lies, because the new quality cannot be maintained, and as the opposition, you become just like the apparatus itself. At some point, it always catches up with you.

Because you're illegal, you can't keep your contact with the people at the base. You no longer take part directly in any further development of the whole scene. You're not integrated with the living process that goes on. Suddenly you're a marginal figure because you can't show up anywhere, you're not directly in it, in the general process, to the same extent.

Consequently, the group becomes increasingly closed. The greater the pressure from the outside, the more you stick together, the more mistakes you make, the more pressure is turned inward—somewhere you have to even things out.

What did people in at the end were the psychological difficulties inside the group. They appear everywhere, but you can diminish them if you have a larger spectrum toward the outside, or learning processes, where sometimes strangers are present too—someone you can talk to about how things are going. That's how it was with all the communes.

But you can't do that anymore. You can't bring some chick back to your pad, because it's illegal, no one is allowed to know about it. That was a problem too, that most of us didn't have a woman. I was always very lucky, I usually did have a woman. But most of our group didn't have that anymore. They ran around for the whole year without seeing a woman. That's a terrific stress, you really have to picture that. Just those who began with sexual revolution and so on—none of that takes place anymore. It's all written off, because you run into a bank, or deliver some leaflet, or throw a bomb somewhere, and run around with a gun in your pocket.

You start developing the instincts of an animal of prey. After a while, you just run around like a gunman. Any sharp eye could recognize you. It's crazy what you do, always running around with a gun. A man who runs around with a gun anchors his center on the weapon—where you carry it, that's your center, you move so that you can always pull it out any time, anywhere. Today, I can tell with anyone if he's got a gun on him, and where he has it, because you can see how he moves.

This crazy concentration, all day long, those are all the things that come together horribly at the end, when there's no more sensibility in the group. Only rigid continuation, total pressure to achieve, and it keeps going, always gets worse, until at some point, some guy collapses—he just can't go along with it anymore, he can't do it. At the end, Brockmann was green in the face, he was pouring down coffee and speed in order to go on. Pure heaps of speed—they can only go on with pills, before they collapse somewhere, or stop completely, or lose it completely; they can't check out what's going on, and just run around loose, shooting at people. There's only this possibility at the end, that's what makes the thing so heavy, and that's where failure lies.

You only have contact with other people as objects, when you meet somebody all you can say is, listen old man, you have to get me this or that thing, rent me a place to live, here or there, and in three days we'll meet here at this corner. If he has any criticism of you, you say, that doesn't interest me at all. Either you participate, or you leave it, easy and clear. At the end it's caught up with you—you become like the apparatus you fight against.

Support Through So-called Sympathizers

Then later, there was a tendency in the left to say, R.A.F. isn't a political group anymore, because they no longer take part in any political dialogues. It was said they'd become criminals, who rob banks and live in expensive apartments, and drive around in expensive cars. It was after this that R.A.F. laid its bombs, in order to legitimatize itself again as a political group; out of this emergency situation they started their insane bombing campaign, which was really wrong.

They made the same mistake in large that we had made two years earlier in small form. They threw bombs suddenly, not against a specific target, but against God and the world—police, Americans, judges, Springer. In the process, of course, they made large mistakes, and blew up workers at Springer. And that's when the real turnabout happened, a total falling away, people really started to withold their support.

That made it difficult for us too. Comrades were saying, not anymore, now it's over. Some of them threatened us openly with the police. They said, you can walk out of here now, but if you stay, we'll call the bulls—it actually happened to me.

And it happened to R.A.F. too. Their stories of betrayal always involved their liberal sympathizers, who informed on them. They were all betrayed within a week, all of them by their so-called sympathizers, with whom they had only this object-relationship.

The interview in the *Spiegel* with the apprentice printer who informed on Ingrid Moeller and Juenschke is particularly significant. He said that he only regretted it with Ingrid, because she still met with him at times just to have a cup of coffee, that is, to have simple, normal contact with him.

This was never checked out. In the final analysis you can't blame the man. That's how everything went, those are exactly the mistakes that happened.

R.A.F. said the revolution wouldn't be built through political work, but through headlines, through appearances in the press, over and over again, reporting: 'Here are guerrillas fighting in Germany.' This overestimation of the press, that's where it completely falls apart. Not only do they have to imitate the machine completely, and fall into the trap of only getting into it politically with the police, but their only justification comes through the media. They establish themselves only by these means.

Things only float at this point, they aren't rooted anymore in anything, not even in the people they still have contact with; those are actually the breaks in the story where you get hung up, apart from the bad vibes inside the group itself.

Terror-Zentrale ausgehoben
Bei „Bethanien" eingerückt

TERRORIST CENTER CLEARED OUT
IN RAID NEAR 'BETHANIEN'

Officers of the Special and Criminal Police began a massive raid today in the early morning hours at the so-called "Georg von Rauch House," occupied by youths for some time in the area of the Bethanien Hospital in Kreuzberg. Approximately 400 officers surrounded the building at Mariannen Place, 1A, and searched the rooms. A spokesman for the Political Police reported to *Der Abend* at the close of the action that "evidence of crimes with explosives of recent times was taken into custody."

from *Der Abend*

Massive raid early this morning at the 'Georg von Rauch House.'

Among them, according to the information of the spokesman, were also those who were connected with the bombing attack on the British Yacht Club in Kladow on the 2nd of February in which the 66-year old German boatbuilder was killed.

The police observed the residents of the Georg von Rauch House during the investigation into the explosive and arson hits of the last few months. In relation to this, the police reported early today that it came to their attention that fire extinguishers of the same kind as those used in the attack on the British Yacht club were stored. In addition, a "prepared pipe" was found in which it was presumably a case of the same explosives which were used in the attack on the B.V.G. Building on Potsdamer Street.

The massive action was conducted early at 4:00 AM this morning, as a result of a decision by the Administrative Court in Tiergarten, "in the framework of preliminary proceedings into the murder of the boatbuilder Irwin Beelitz." According to the first announcement of the Political Police, 63 persons were in the building at the time of the raid. 27 of them were temporarily taken into custody on suspicion of having committed various crimes, among them, crimes with explosives and i.d. falsifications. Their interrogations were still going on at the time *Abend* went to press.

As was reported, the Political Police for some time has had the suspicion that the recent bombing attacks were all carried out by the same Anarchist group.

HES Berlin, April 19

Bei Fahndung nach der Baader-Meinhof-Bande:

Freund Georg von Rauchs in Augsburg von einem Polizeibeamten erschossen

Eine junge Frau festgenommen – Kripo: Beide wollten schießen

In the Search for the Baader-Meinhof Band:

A FRIEND OF GEORG VON RAUCH SHOT IN AUGSBURG BY POLICE OFFICER

Young woman taken into custody: Both wanted to shoot.

Augsburg, March 3

During a search for members of the Baader-Meinhof band, the 23-year old Thomas Weisbecker from Freiburg in Breisgau was shot yesterday at noon in Augsburg by an officer of the Special Commission of the Bavarian Provincial Office of Criminal Police. A woman was taken into custody. Weisbecker was a friend of Georg von Rauch, who was shot in Berlin under circumstances which have not yet been fully explained.

Thomas Weisbecker, born February 24, 1949 in Freiburg, the son of a professor, died shortly after he was delivered to a hospital. The officer who shot him has, according to the police, just recently received special training in "Combat shooting." As the police further reported, Weisbecker immediately grabbed for his pistol as two officers attempted to question him. The policeman shot as the young man directed his weapon toward one of the officers. There were two arrest warrants against Weisbecker from the Berlin Court, for dangerous bodily injury, dangerous arson, and resisting arrest.

**Thomas
Weisbecker**

The dead man is supposed to have belonged to a marginal group of the Baader-Meinhof band. Until he went underground, he made headlines above all in Berlin. He is suspected of having taken part in arson attacks on the America House, and KaDaWe. His most spectacular criminal act: In July, 1971, he helped Georg von Rauch in his escape from Moabit Criminal Court. Weisbecker, who looked like von Rauch, sat down at the defense table so that von Rauch's disappearance from the courtroom was noticed too late. Weisbecker participated too in the attack on a journalist from the illustrated "Quick."

Thomas Weisbecker and a young woman had been watched by the police for some time now. Officers of the Special Commission of the Bavarian Provincial Criminal Police had rented a place four weeks ago in the vicinity of the house in Augsberg in which Weisbecker lived with the woman. Yesterday noon, Weisbecker was stopped in the vicinity of the Augsburg City Works as he was headed toward his parked Audi sedan. The car had a phony license plate. The young woman was within calling distance of the 23-year old. She also attempted to pull a pistol, according to the police report. She ran about a hundred meters before she could be overpowered with "great resistance," and could be taken into custody, and brough to the police station.

The young woman carried a large sum of money bundled in thousand Mark bills, and like Weisbecker carried on her a 9mm pistol. Her identity is not yet known. During her booking, she said "not a single word," according to police reports.

Some Disguises

CHAPTER ELEVEN

Terror or Love?

Making a decision for terrorism is something already psychologically programmed. Today, I can see that—for myself —it was only the fear of love, from which one flees into absolute violence. If I had checked out the dimension of love for myself beforehand, I wouldn't have done it. I would have recognized it correctly, in a roundabout way.

The only time I was in the process of recognizing it was during my relationship with Hella. But that's when I went to the joint. That's the breaks again. The joint can produce only hate—and later she was destroyed by the pigs while she was sick in bed, to cause even more hatred.

This was actually true with many, in fact, with everybody. It always showed in the sexual relationships they had. The old anarchist Malatesta found it out, and Fromm proved it psychoanalytically: fear of freedom exists in the mass psychology. Fear is based on ignorance. When you don't *know* anymore, you become fearful because of your upbringing. I saw the fear of love in these things in the same way: it does exist.

I saw that with a great many, in very specific things, when it really got serious, they did things sloppily, or they took on bourgeois ways of being, and they continued to be the same dim-witted oppressors of women or hardheaded bulls.

Everyone fell apart over these things: Brockmann is a prime example. As a result of all this stress, and because at the end he was just running around for the group like a delivery boy—he was an employee again—his girl friend Petra had become his last connection. I knew her too. When he realized he was going to lose her because of all this stuff, he decided in favor of her. That was actually the last clear thing he did, and then he got caught, and collapsed.

When the bulls say, listen, either you inform, or your chick's gonna disappear, you'll never see her again—at that moment he simply says, okay, here, I'll tell you what I know, from A to Z, without mercy. No one is to blame for that; you really have to see it that way. Brockmann is not a traitor in the classical sense: he is really only a victim of circumstance.

These points—fear of love, and fear of freedom—really have to be taken into account, and have to be worked at.

For example, with these young boys in the Rauch House, the primary thing is the fear of freedom. When they don't know what to do, they go back to the factory to work—they can't handle this new-won freedom which for them has really come overnight; they don't know what to do anymore. They let themselves be persuaded, and go back to the factory again, instead of finding creative forms of life, through which they could find a common ground.

We overcame the fear of freedom, and immediately ran into the next problem: fear of love. Our mistakes helped to further that. These are the central psychological concepts which surfaced in the midst of things, and they have to be worked at, so that new things can develop.

Until now, it has been assumed that there is no simultaneity of revolutionary praxis and love. I don't see that, even today I don't. Otherwise, I might have continued. But I saw it like this: you make your decision, and you stop and throw away your gun, and say: okay—the end.

For me, the whole time it was a question of creating human values which did not exist in capitalism, in all of Europe, in all of Western culture—they'd been cleared away by the machine. That's what it's about: to discover them anew, to unfold them anew, and to create them anew. In that way, too, you carry the torch again, you become the bearer of a new society—if it is possible. And you'll be better doing that than bombing it in, creating the same rigid figures of hatred at the end. Stalin was actually a type like us: he made it, one of the few who made it. But then it got heavy.

You can see how bad it was in Schmuecker's case—they shot him down. He was just a small, harmless student. They forced him into one of these situations, not asking themselves if he was far enough along to handle it? He couldn't have talked that much anyway, and then they did him in. That's real destruction;

you just can't see it any other way. The murder of Schmuecker reminds one strongly of Charles Manson. It really is murder, you have to see that. They threatened me with that too, but I just laughed at it. But a guy like Schmuecker, they just wrap him up and do him in.

This Book Is Meant To Be A Contribution

If you have to choose between the bomb and love, and only love emerges in that choice, that is first of all completely private and nothing is changed: it remains limited to itself. But then you can translate that too, and you get power from the other side, which you can put to new use, so that you can speak and communicate with people again in a different way. Other things get started simply from a different viewpoint. It doesn't necessarily have to be an armed thing, because in that form it isn't possible, the conditions just aren't there at the moment; there's no alternative to be seen. It's only a matter of keeping the fire going; at the moment you can't do anymore than that.

If I do a book like this one—as honestly as possible—I believe it will help people to think once again about how it all went, and how it could actually go. That's a contribution, too, a way that you can take part in the process as up-front and as self-critically as you can, even if some people don't like it, because a lot is being said which many will take badly.

I personally see a general development in the elimination of old processes, so that something new is developed: for example, this commune business. There are other social analyses that have been added: drugs, for example, have created other dimensions which can be utilized differently; the business of children is new; several things have been added which could be further developed. A different relationship to technology has been created.

All these years should be reflected upon. The well-traveled roads that exist now, there's nothing progressive about them anymore. As true for some M-L faction as for some student group still reading Mr. Marx—that just doesn't make it anymore.

It's a question of thinking up new forms. I don't have a message; I can't really say it. There's stagnation in the whole movement everywhere; it shows itself wherever in the world anything like this was happening. Everyone is thinking about it; this stagnation is a worldwide phenomenon. Everyone is touched by it. Right now, it's the best thing, for those who have been at it for a long time, to reflect once more on the events, maybe something will still come out of it.

For me it looks like this: I never carried on this business of love correctly, and now I'm really going through it; first because it's fun and it's good, and because after all these heavy years I need it.

Generally you can say, if you've already reached a stage like this and it's going smoothly for you, and you're politically active, maybe even in terrorism, you can probably bring it off on a much more thorough and cooler lever. If we had all been people like that, I mean if our structures had already settled to that extent before we started all this stuff, then of course all these irrational things would never have happened. At that point you're a much more mature type. There would have been fewer informants too; it would have been much more humane. Many things would have appeared on the scene in a better way.

Then revolution wouldn't be made as a result of hatred, or of pressure to achieve, out of disappointment and the like, but by bringing about a humane society quietly and considerately— something already laid out within one's self. Not a totally abstract theory. Things would be actualized in a better way, and many things would be dealt with better.

Even if violence were used then, it would have a much more real connection, and would most probably be carried out better. This process can still develop now, and it will, and it too will certainly find its nadir.

To See the Movement as a Totality

Perhaps one should also attempt to see the whole movement as a totality.

When people go to the country, because of problems in the environment, and dig up new things there, or even go to India and sit under the palms with a guru for half a year, they can bring good things back with them, different processes. Of course, when it becomes an ideology or a message, then naturally it gets heavy too. All that is still a part of the movement. Either it's everybody, or it's nobody; anything else is a splintering. You have to see it as a whole story, as the story that started after the second World War, in all its breadth.

Everyone who has experiences and translates them makes his contribution on whatever level. If one works in a daycare center, the other stands on the barricades with his gun, the third brings back a pound of hashish from India, or some Mick Jagger dances so wildly on the stage that everyone goes crazy; everyone has a part in this process. I see it as a total story.

If you look at any one thing in isolation, and say, this is the only thing that's true, then it becomes one of these trips. They're all knights of the grail, they all protect the grail, but whether the grail exists at all is really the question.

One should look at the whole thing as hanging together from the beginning, from Hemingway's 'lost generation,' through the beatniks, to today. It's about survival. Therefore, one should look at everything, find what's positive, and develop that further. Not only from a Marxist viewpoint, which always says this thing is petit-bourgeois, that's bourgeois, this is lumpenproletarian, that's individualistic, this is objectivistic, this is positivistic, this is empirical—which is really only one standpoint, the Marxist one. So that really won't get us anywhere.

Progress was made everywhere. Mistakes were made in the process, but it was only at that price that the experiences were to be gained. From there, new levels can be reached.

Illegality Now—Outside the Group—A Life Without a Past

For many, it's like this: it's assumed that one can only continue, or get shot, or go to the joint, and that there's nothing outside of that.

The roads of retreat are all closed; one blows up all the bridges behind one in the truest sense of the word.

But even here, there's still a way out: a) because in the meantime, one has become skilled at falsifying papers, one never has difficulties, so one is better off than all the other illegals in the world, because out of nothing we can make the papers ourselves; and b) the thing is this, that when you start to go a different way, alternatives immediately open up.

You lead a life without a past, living without a personal history. That's exactly the situation for you. You're exactly the person you are at that moment. No history follows you anymore. That's when it first gets interesting, when you live in illegality, because it has advantages. You can't be integrated into the bourgeois system anymore, you're always outside, you're not burdened with a thousand prejudices, you've stepped into a completely new interim zone; of course very few people are doing that at this time. I can only say, it's really a good thing.

You start to count as someone, your personality structure functions from a new level. You gain completely new insights. You withdraw yourself from persecution stress. When you step out of a group like this, you can't be found by the bulls; then it's over. You've made it, it's a good condition; one can't recommend it to everybody, because the road there is a very hard one, but it has its advantages.

Naturally you still have to be careful. You can move in all the scenes—not only in the left, which is so often studded with spies, and where you have to be the person you *were*. You don't have to appear as the persecuted terrorist—that's wrong; that trip will follow you eternally. You'll never get rid of it. People like Bakunin, these old people who ran through the world with just this kind of karma, and never got rid of it. You can start a completely new thing.

For me personally, this was added to it: I saw that one day I would continue to fight, on a different level, in a different area. That's the way it is. You can't escape that karma. Don't fool yourself about that; at some point, I will step into the fight again, but on a completely different level.

I still stand behind all the things I have done. I don't condemn anything, and I don't judge anything wrong, not the people either, even if I criticize. I still like them just as much, even the worst bigots, who at the moment all wish me the worst.

I did it, and it's all right. Even the worst experiences were right in their time, because otherwise, it wouldn't have come to this point. That was your road, and you had to walk it.

22jähriger Student im Grunewald erschossen

22 YEAR OLD STUDENT SHOT IN GRUNEWALD

Was the student Ulrich Schmuecker killed by Anarchists in Grunewald? The 22-year old was found with a fatal head wound. He previously belonged to a terrorist group.

Annerose Reiche   Inge Viett   Ralf Reinders   Norbert Krocher

Michael Baumann   Werner Sauber   Till Meyer   Peter Knoll

WANTED: ANARCHISTS

I Don't Have a Message

I've told my story, and it should be understood as one among many, as *my* contribution, how I see the thing now, from the experiences I've had and the way I've digested them. Of course it has no universal validity. All criticisms contained in this book are also intended solely to let others measure their trips against them, to learn from the experiences and mistakes that were made. Others should understand why people take the road of armed struggle, how they come to it, how the seeds are planted, and what the emotions behind it are, what kind of considerations and psychic preconditions are needed to overcome the fear involved.

Basically it's a completely normal Berlin Blues Story that became significant simply because it went beyond the boundaries that had previously been established; in other words, it wasn't just verbal protest anymore but a serious attempt to bring about change through force of arms. Although the attempt failed it was correct and useful.

I don't say that because I'm smarter than others or have turned overnight into a pacifist. For a long time I believed that urban guerrilla war was the best way and I tried to describe here my development into a guerrilla and to explain why I've now decided for something else.

I should mention that even before the appearance of this book, and especially after the spectacular Lorenz abduction [see chronology]—a real masterwork of urban guerrilla action—voices were raised that wanted to shorten it or even stop publication.

The call to throw away the gun is seen by the revolutionaries as compromise or even as betrayal. It should be understood, though, as a turning towards a constructive concept, an opening up to new insights and experiments, an effort to maintain life so we don't get buried in the rubble of the collapsing system. The other side thinks about extermination often enough.

> *So many roads so many trains to ride*
> *I am standing on my window.**

---

*Source unknown.

DANIEL COHN-BENDIT

A Statement

If I associate myself with the publication of this book, if I support it, it is not only on account of its vital contribution to current realities, but indeed because I identify with it completely and regard it, in contrast to some others, as a literary masterpiece. It strikes me as truly exceptional when a writer succeeds in transmitting to others a part of his consciousness—that is, when the words do not interpose themselves between him and the reader like a screen or a mask. Just the opposite: one discovers the author with all the contradictions he brings with him and which he will have to acknowledge right to the end. Bommi's situation doesn't allow him to say to us: 'Hey you guys, here I am, Bommi Baumann, here's my story.' He isn't free; he's being hunted by the police in this country.

The final chapter of the book, entitled 'Terrorism or Love'—the content of which has been violently attacked by the German Left, although not by the German Security Police—possesses, for me, a primary significance. The criticisms which say, 'one doesn't talk like *that* about love' aren't convincing. The fact that someone has the courage to say that—to say yes to love and no to hatred—as the principal motivation for political action seems to me an essential statement in this book, a revolutionary one.

Whatever political strategy one might choose today, it seems to me that it is doomed to fail utterly if it doesn't take into consideration this essential dimension of life. This is why the appearance of this book possesses, in my opinion, such importance. Of course, there are legal issues as well—the political suppression of this work by this country's authorities—but our most important task is to distribute it as widely as possible because it is a revolutionary book, a helpful tool for turning society over. It must come out, be sold and spread around in thousands of copies. Whatever means the authorities may use to suppress the free circulation of the book, we will find others to get it to the public. We won't be short of ideas. The recent Swedish translation is an example—now it's up to Olaf Palme to ban its distribution. It is about to be published in France as well, in a series edited by Jean-Paul Sartre. Recall the cynical, tedious reactions of the German press on the occasion of the Baader-Sartre conference in Stuttgart! The *Welt* [right-wing German daily], an honourable journal as everyone knows, reported that this 'Gentleman' had been a terrorist for years—after all, hadn't he urged his countrymen to bomb the German army in W.W.II? Hadn't he already called for insurrection right in the middle of a war? What a monster!

We are now at the very heart of the matter: violence. I consider that Bommi's book, which frankly poses the problem, makes a significant contribution to that discussion. I'm going to choose a commonplace example from current politics in this country to illustrate. Voerster is received here by Willy Brandt and Chancellor Schmidt. It is pure and simple cynicism that declares on such an occasion: 'Don't worry, we're quite able to tell him just what we think of his apartheid policy.' Hasn't history sufficiently shown us the perversity of this brand of politics? To receive a Hitler, make him presentable through diplomatic channels, all the while criticizing him, springs from the absurd. To say to this sort of individual: 'Listen, your politics don't please us much, but even so, here's a few billions for you.' That's what makes a few hundred guys freak out. The high-sounding talk won't satisfy anymore, nothing works, there are only bombs.

Leave a bomb at the South African Travel Bureau—it's the only thing that can soothe in a case like that! Who hasn't dreamed of kidnapping Voerster and handing him over to the Blacks of the Johannesburg ghettoes? Who hasn't contemplated it? I ask you. As far as I'm concerned, precisely the one who hasn't is the true criminal, whereas the one who has thought of it is good, a real human being.

Bommi speaks about all this in his book, and it's why it was vital that it be published: it is also why we will continue the struggle to assure its distribution.

But let's get back to its suppression. I am opposed to all

banning of books or films, regardless of content. For I am convinced that contradictions are resolved by discussion, not by censorship. So let the right-wing press ramble on! If we can't dissuade the people from reading it, suppression would be useless. Don't forget the history of the revolutionary workers' movement: in all times there have been groups and factions who talk of liberty but whose practice has been completely otherwise—I allude here to the communist parties of socialist countries. Will we lose all credibility if we keep silent about W. Biermann and R. Havermann? [East-German intellectuals prosecuted for their continuous criticism of the communist system in East Germany]. To struggle like we do against the wretched treatment dealt to our comrades imprisoned here in Germany requires that we equally denounce the condition of prisoners in Czechoslovakia. Whoever forgets to fight for Plioutch and his comrades* in the U.S.S.R., rotting in psychiatric hospitals, hasn't the right to speak here. Equally, to battle for them requires that we fight against censure here at home.

I insist that I'm not speaking for myself alone but on behalf of a whole segment of the anti-capitalist, anti-authoritarian movement in Germany. I presume that we have a responsibility which we do not have the right to renounce. We will not let ourselves get stuck in the perennial argument about liberty-repression. We are sustained solely by Utopia, the permanent motive of our actions—by the desire and thirst for freedom. That is why we do not keep silent when it comes to Bommi's book or anyone else's.

In closing, a word about the German press, because it is perhaps the most demoralizing factor of all. Books are banned in France, too. I still remember—I was very young at the time—my brother passing me a banned book under his coat: *La Question* by Henri Alleg, which described torture in Algeria. It isn't so much a question of whether this or that state apparatus is more or less odious, but simply of stressing that there exists in France and Sweden a class of intellectuals and liberal democrats who sometimes dare to rise against censorship, whereas here in Germany we are constrained to fight simultaneously against the combined might of the media and state apparatus. Only a few weeks ago, in June 1976, the television broadcast, in Frankfurt,

*Political prisoners in the U.S.S.R.

the photos of eight of our comrades accused of having participated in a violent rally. They were denounced as 'leaders' who tossed molotov cocktails, and styled as assassins. People were asked to come and testify against them! Nobody responded to this appeal since everyone had taken part in the demonstration. Of course, they have been freed, but what really hurts is that no one protested, and the situation was permitted to dissolve into apathy.

We are always waiting for the journalists to decide to denounce this censorship in their respective newspapers— suppression which, we know full well, exists. But no one budges; each seems to have a ready excuse. This is the greatest danger in Germany today. That a book is suppressed, that's nothing new, but that responsible people in the media accept it...that strikes me as ominous. Precisely this, in my opinion, is the point of our political discussion today. If we succeed in breaking the massive coalition of political parties, police and journalists' administrations, to create active public opinion outside these factions, we will win the fight against the fascist elements in today's Germany.

Bommi Baumann's book plays an important part in this struggle. Will the authorities, perhaps, ban it yet again? We'll cheer every move they make in that direction: it will enable us to circulate several thousand more copies.

Daniel Cohn-Bendit was known as Red Danny in the 1968 uprisings in France. He came to be one of the better known voices of the '60's anti-authoritarian political scene in Europe, and was deported from France back to Germany because of his prominant role in the 'almost revolution.'

This statement was first given at a press conference organized in July 1976 by Trikont Verlag to protest the seizure of Bommi's book.

HEINRICH BÖLL

A Statement

To confiscate this book and attempt to suppress it, and to prosecute Trikont for its publication is the worst possible course one could take. One should work, rather, towards its wide circulation and recommend it for (non-obligatory) school use—with commentary, of course. And to apply thoroughly, for once, the idiot-demand for 'balanced reporting' one should allow it to be commented on—by someone from the Right, someone from the Left, someone from the Middle, someone from the Middle of the Middle, by a Protestant, by a Catholic, by a Christian and by a representative from each of those parties not represented in the Parliament.

If I ignore the few (there weren't many) inveterate objections and a few (not many) hot-headed denunciations, and conclude—without being able to prove it—that the book is authentic, I find that I have rarely read anything so revealing from the Underground. We're listening here to one of those rare birds about which the abstract (and occasionally arrogant) intellectual Left has so often and intensively dreamed—an actual *worker*. Baumann tells the story of his development, first into a personal, later an organized anarchism: oppressive living conditions; unhappy domestic situation; the sudden realization of the young worker that the treadmill stretches out forty or fifty years ahead of him. Escape into the commune; insights gained there; and then the incredible ease with which he slips into making bombs, almost as a game at first, later in earnest.

I cannot imagine that a young person who is not already, and without any prodding, attracted to the idea of 'Mollies' or bombs would be led on by this book; not more so, at least, than he is led on by the tough-guy, shoot-from-the-hip westerns he is allowed to admire almost daily on television—those violent, hard men-of-action who are so often held as examples. 'Anti-radical,' 'anti-extremist' legislation—it is these atrocities that will drive hundreds if not thousands of youths into the Underground; and not only those presently banned from 'public service' but also those who, as a result of the actively circulating blacklists, have become 'unmanageable' in the private sector as well. Let responsibility for their ensuing plans, their possible actions rest with those parties who 'manage' such legislation. There'll be a number of things to 'manage': such legislation does more to breed radicals, extremists, potential terrorists than it ever does to hinder them. There'll be ample copy for the columnists and headline writers of the sensationalist press. Perhaps one needs the extremists, needs to nurture them in this way in order to bring down tighter and tighter laws. Those who are relegated to the Underground by *legal means* will develop entirely different forms and analyses, entirely different frustrations than those who, like Michael Baumann, chose illegality from the outset. For these people Baumann cannot be an example, because they had initially wanted to work within the law, within the social framework.

Michael Baumann *explains* a lot, in his own way, and, as the bourgeois stylist that I remain, I cannot always tell if his tone is not sometimes artificially flippant. He explains 'how it all began.' How it ended we learn from the book itself. The *Spiegel* interview had given us a foretaste: 'With Beelitz (a victim of one of Baumann's bombs) we got a shock; with Georg von Rauch we learned hate.' Baumann adds a few comments to that interview: 'The Left has made a real Christian martyr—a real Christian humanity trip is what's coming off. The guy wasn't like that, he was the kind of guy who said, of course we'll shoot.' Whether or not von Rauch really shot first doesn't become clear from these comments. Baumann writes further: 'Already once before Urbach had given us weapons; thus the Security Police delivered weapons with which the police would be shot down.'

The active resort to violence, conscious violence (even for Baumann) did not come until after the shooting of Ohnesorg and the attempt on Dutschke. The other contributing factor was —and one cannot emphasize this often enough—the sensation-mongering of the Springer Press, especially in Berlin where it controls the market and intimidates those markets it doesn't control. Perhaps one day a group of researchers will retrace the step-by-step, day-by-day development of this press violence and counter-violence. One cannot dissociate the violence in which Baumann became involved from this context of sensationalism, hate campaigns, and incitements of public opinion. Let Michael Baumann, if he is captured, be faced with the responsibility for his actions as the written law decrees: the laws against press violence and manipulation remain unwritten and without a judge or a courtroom.

Baumann, in reference to the members of his group from proletarian backgrounds, writes: 'We'd lived with violence from the time we were children; it has material roots. On payday, when the old man comes home drunk and beats up the old lady —it's all that stuff. At school, you get into fights, you have to make your way with fists, for you that's a perfectly normal thing; you fight at your workplace, you fight in bars, you have a more healthy relationship to it. For you, violence is a completely spontaneous thing that you can unroll quite easily. There was always this split between the R.A.F. and ourselves about the source of violence, where it was coming from.'

The chapter 'Terror or Love?' begins: 'Making a decision for terrorism is something already programmed. Today I can see that—for myself—it was only the fear of love, from which one flees into absolute violence. If I had checked out the dimension of love for myself beforehand, I wouldn't have done it. I would have recognized it correctly, in a roundabout way.' These are direct, bold, revealing statements. (One could quote many similar passages.) For their sake alone the book should be widely distributed and read. Sexual oppression or repressed sexuality—Baumann correctly calls it *love*—where else can one find clearer, more direct insight into the connection between these forces and terrorism? And these statements, some of which have a lyrical quality, are nowhere, not even for my bourgeois sensibility, even remotely 'obscene.'

In Baumann's testimony there are few excuses, some regrets, and everything is *explained*—not from the point of view of theory, but from an analysis of and insight into praxis, experience, historical background, and personal development. This book should be read by teachers, parents, politicians and psychologists, police officers and priests to expand their insights and provide information. I recommend it also for young people who, perhaps from a sense of boredom, are *toying* with Underground and anarchist ideas. I especially recommend a careful look at the photo of the clean-cut, well-dressed, 'nice' young worker, Michael Baumann, and I hope, wherever he may be, that he has a young 'bride.'

Heinrich Böll is a famous civil libertarian novelist. He is generally considered to be the best contemporary writer in West Germany and won the Nobel Prize for Literature in 1972.

This statement first appeared in the journal Konkret, *in February, 1976, as 'Voice from the Underground.'*
